ETHICS IN CLINICAL PSYCHOLOGY

ETHICS
IN
CLINICAL PSYCHOLOGY

JANE STEERE

1984 OXFORD UNIVERSITY PRESS CAPE TOWN

Oxford University Press
OXFORD LONDON NEW YORK
TORONTO MELBOURNE AUCKLAND NAIROBI
DAR ES SALAAM CAPE TOWN KUALA LUMPUR
SINGAPORE HONG KONG TOKYO DELHI
BOMBAY CALCUTTA MADRAS KARACHI

AND ASSOCIATES IN
BEIRUT BERLIN IBADAN MEXICO CITY NICOSIA

ISBN 0 19 570373 1

OXFORD is a trademark of Oxford University Press

Printed and bound by Citadel Press, Lansdowne, Cape
Published by Oxford University Press, Harrington House,
Barrack Street, Cape Town 8001, South Africa

CONTENTS

PREFACE

The question of what constitutes ethical behaviour for clinical psychologists in their diverse areas of functioning is one which has attracted a great deal of attention in professional literature. Well-researched and carefully drafted ethical codes have been developed by professional organizations for psychologists in many countries, but it is apparent from discussion and debate in the literature that these codes are often limited in their usefulness. Their limitations arise partly from their brevity, which disallows a full discussion of the merits and demerits of various courses of action, and partly from their failure to provide guidance as to how to behave when two or more ethical regulations come into conflict.

The process of ethical decision-making for clinical psychologists therefore involves far more than a routine adherence to the rules contained within professional ethical codes, and demands a careful consideration of the ethical issues at stake in every individual situation. The purpose of this book is to facilitate this process of ethical decision-making by clarifying the essential ethical principles of which all psychologists must be aware and by illustrating how these principles, when applied to practical situations, determine ethically appropriate behaviour.

Discussion within the book falls into two major sections. The first section introduces the philosophical study of ethics and identifies the major areas of functioning of clinical psychologists, while the second section is concerned with the application of ethical principles to practical situations with which clinical psychologists may be faced. Specific attention is given to the areas of psychotheraphy, psychological assessment, research, professional conduct and the psychologist's involvement in legal processes. The final chapter addresses the unique circumstances pertaining to clinical psychologists practising in South Africa and examines the ethical issues raised by the socio-political situation in this country.

Ethical decision-making will never be an easy task for clinical psychologists and will continue to demand intelligent and objective appraisal of the issues relevant to particular circumstances, but it is hoped that this book will go some way towards alerting practising psychologists to the kinds of issues which need to be borne in mind in ethically complex situations. An awareness of such issues and willingness to take cognizance of them in all circumstances is essential for the welfare of the clinical psychologist's client population and thereby for the standing of the profession as a whole.

ACKNOWLEDGEMENTS

Special thanks to Terry Dowdall, director of the U.C.T. Child Guidance Clinic, for his invaluable guidance, advice and assistance with the original work on which this book is based.

Thanks also to Professor Gustav Fouché, Professor Dave Beyers, Tony Morphet, Kim Meyer and June Coutts, for their advice and assistance.

Financial support for the publication of this book was generously granted by the University of Cape Town.

INTRODUCTION

During the course of day-to-day living, every individual is faced with a constant series of choices between alternative courses of action. The decision as to which course to take appears to be generally guided by two major considerations. The first consideration may be seen as self-interest – that is, which action one desires, or would *like* to choose – while the second consideration is what is generally termed conscience or a sense of moral duty – that is, which action one *should* choose, or which would be the *right* thing to do in a particular situation. This latter consideration in human decision-making is the subject matter of the philosophical study of ethics which is concerned with the process by which certain forms of conduct come to be defined as 'good' or 'bad' within human societies, and organized into sets of rules or codes of ethics which regulate interaction within these societies.

THE PURPOSE AND NATURE OF ETHICAL CODES

The major purpose of sets of moral laws is to ensure the smooth and harmonious functioning of society. Ideally, they provide an external, objective set of criteria whereby individual actions which threaten the desired social harmony may be judged, punished and prevented, thereby providing protection and a sense of security to individuals who may within a safe environment contribute positively towards the well-being and progress of all within the community.

Because these kinds of laws arise within a community or society, they are most frequently expressed in terms of behaviour within relationships between people, stipulating the relative roles and responsibilities which are demanded of each individual within particular relationships. It is apparent that the kinds of applicable laws will differ according to the specific type of relationship and the context within which this relationship exists, so that for example, the rules for marital relationships will be different from those for friends or father and son. Generally speaking, the more risk there is of exploitation or harm of one individual by another within a relationship, the more explicit and detailed the rules governing their interaction need to be.

This book is concerned with the particular relationship entered into by the clinical psychologist as professional and his clients. It is obvious that this relationship differs in several important respects from any of the other types of relationships in which either party may be engaged, and it therefore has unique risks of harm and exploitation which need to be reduced and monitored through a set of rules to which each party must adhere. The rules for such interaction form part of a subsection of ethics known as *professional ethics*.

PROFESSIONAL ETHICS

There has been much dispute amongst scholars of varying disciplines as to the exact definition of a 'profession', but it is generally agreed that a profession is primarily an occupation at which an individual, who has been specifically trained to do so, fulfils a task which is desired and valued by society. In other words, a professional performs a service to society as a whole by virtue of his occupational role. Further, a profession claims a particular problem area within society as its domain and, through organization of its individual members, lays down standards by which these members will conduct themselves in addressing this problem area.

Because professions offer a service to society it is essential that they maintain sufficient trust and confidence of members of the public to allow them to pursue their socially-valued ends. For this reason, professional ethical codes which assure the public of certain basic levels of expertise and protection are essential. By devising and enforcing such codes the profession also protects itself from interference by higher law-making bodies such as the state, who may allow the profession to function autonomously with the assurance that the profession will itself protect clients from harm. Thus, such ethical regulations have a two-fold purpose; they protect members of the public from exploitation by professionals and they protect the profession itself from excessive regulation by state institutions which could restrict it in the achievement of aims. Downie (1980) proposes that a professional code should embody three main components:

1. Standards of professional competence
2. Standards of professional integrity
3. Accepted professional procedures;

to which could be added a fourth component in the form of effective mechanisms for ensuring that these standards are maintained by individual practitioners.

It is apparent that clinical psychology is a profession in that it offers a valued service to members of the public and, along with other mental health professions, it delineates the area of mental health as its area of expertise. Clinical psychology must, therefore, have an adequate ethical code which will regulate the conduct of individual practitioners and thereby win and maintain the confidence of the public it is meant to serve. The appropriate contents of such an ethical code form the subject matter of this book.

SOCIETAL ETHICS AND PROFESSIONAL ETHICS

It is apparent that any professional must be subject to two sets of ethical principles – those which are generally held by all members of society and those which are specified by the profession to which he or she belongs. Naturally no professional ethical code can establish rules which violate the general ethical standards of the community, and, for this reason, there are many basic similarities between the principles embodied in professional ethics and those in societal ethics. The major differences concern the principles governing the relationship between people. In general in professional ethics, the over-riding principle is that the clients' interests are given priority above the interests of all others. This is intended to provide assurances to clients that the professional will not allow his own self-interest or the competing claims of others in society to prejudice the client's chances of receiving the best possible treatment. This over-riding principle in professional ethics may however cause conflict between the professional and the broader society when the client's best interests conflict with the best interests of others in society as embodied particularly in the law. The professional's ethical responsibility in such cases poses a tricky question for professional bodies and requires careful regulation. This issue in relation to the profession of clinical psychology is discussed further in following chapters.

CONCLUSION

We have established that the study of ethics is the study of the moral laws which guide human decision-making particularly within relationships. It is apparent that these laws will differ according to the type of relationship which is under consideration, and that the particular type of relationship between the clinical psychologist and his client demands a specific set of rules which are aimed at maintaining trust in the profession, thereby allowing it to perform its function of serving society, by promoting the mental health of members of society.

The types of rules or ethical guidelines which will be appropriate to the practice of clinical psychology will be discussed in this book in two major parts. The first deals with the philosophical basis of ethical decision-making and outlines the development of clinical psychology as a profession, identifying major current areas of functioning of clinical psychologists. Part two is concerned with the application of philosophical ethical principles to these areas and provides guidelines for ethical decision-making in practical situations.

PART ONE

PHILOSOPHICAL ETHICS AND CLINICAL PSYCHOLOGY

This section describes in more detail the philosophical study of ethics and outlines the ethical principles to which clinical psychologists must be committed in their practice. The process of ethical decision-making is outlined, providing guidelines as to the considerations which need to be borne in mind by the practitioner, especially when faced with ethically problematic situations. The development of clinical psychology as a profession is also recorded and the major areas of functioning of clinical psychologists which require ethical regulation are briefly described.

1

THE PROCESS OF ETHICAL DECISION-MAKING

The process of ethical decision-making may be viewed as incorporating two levels of activity. On the first level it involves conforming with specific guidelines for ethical behaviour as set out in rules, while on the second, more complex level, it involves resolving ethical dilemmas – that is, deciding on appropriate conduct where two different rules indicate opposing courses of action. The purpose of this chapter is to examine the way in which ethical rules are derived, to outline the nature of ethical dilemmas, and to propose an approach to the resolution of these dilemmas.

BASIC STRUCTURE OF AN ETHICAL SYSTEM

It has been seen that ethical conduct may be defined as 'good' or 'right' conduct and it stands to reason that, at its most basic level, an ethical system must incorporate a general statement as to what exactly constitutes 'the good'. As yet, there has been no philosophical unanimity on this most basic definition and a number of different ethical theories which hold conflicting views on this issue have been developed over the centuries. In recent years, two major classes of ethical theory have received the most attention. These are the utilitarian and deontological theories, which will be discussed in more detail later in this chapter. At this point, it is merely necessary to note that in general one or the other of these two theories will underlie any system of ethics and will have implications for the process by which ethical decisions are made.

At a second level of conceptualization, an ethical system will make explicit one or more broad ethical principles out of which specific rules may be derived. Ethical principles are general ethical statements which may be encompassed within the underlying ethical theory. A simplistic example of an ethical principle would be a statement such as 'honesty is the best policy' which provides a broad statement of attitude which can then be translated into rules for differing situations.

3

The final level incorporated within an ethical system is the level of rules, which are guidelines for ethical behaviour in relation to others in the environment, for example, rules based on the ethical principle of 'honesty' may be those such as 'you must not lie', 'do not steal', etc. Figure 1 illustrates this underlying structure of an ethical system.

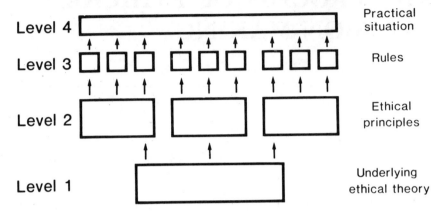

FIG. 1 : Underlying structure of an Ethical System

In order for an ethical system to be coherent and comprehensive, therefore, any rule for conduct must be specifically derived from an ethical principle which is in turn encompassed within the basic ethical theory.

At this point, it may be useful to examine more closely the nature of these essential components of an ethical system.

ETHICAL THEORIES

The first step in proposing a procedure for ethical decision-making is to make a choice between the utilitarian and deontological ethical theories as to which will be regarded as the theory underlying the ethical system as a whole. It is not within the scope of this book to provide a detailed critique of the philosophical validity of either of these two theories. Consequently, they will each be accepted at face value and an attempt will be made only to outline their most significant assumptions and differences.

UTILITARIAN THEORIES

Also sometimes referred to as 'consequentionalist' theories, these theories assert that there is only one important and relevant ethical principle, which is the directive to, in all circumstances, 'maximize the good'. While there have

4

been numerous arguments as to the definition of 'the good' within these theories, the most popular recent definition has been that 'the good' relates to the preference of the individual in specific situations. (Beauchamp and Childress, 1983.) This implies that all actions are judged according to the degree to which they maximize the potential for all individuals affected by the action to realize their preferences.

Two important features of these theories are immediately apparent: firstly, it is the consequence of an action rather than the nature of that action itself which is important; secondly, the consequence of an action is to be evaluated according to its effects on all people involved, rather than according to its effects on one or two individuals. It is these aspects of utilitarian theory which have evoked most criticism in philosophical circles. If actions are to be judged in this way, it is conceivable that behaviours such as lying and killing, which are counter to most people's conceptualizations of 'moral' behaviour, may be condoned, should they have 'good' consequences for a sufficient number of people. In addition, trust in social relationships would be eroded if contracts and promises between individuals could be easily broken where such behaviour would, in utilitarian terms, 'maximize the good'.

Partly as a reaction to this kind of criticism a different form of utilitarianism has evolved which recognizes the value of rules which may not be broken. This version of utilitarianism, known as 'rule utilitarianism' argues that systems of rules have overall utility because they ensure the ordered functioning of society.

Rule utilitarians therefore assert that, rather than judge each individual action according to its consequences, rules should be derived by considering the general utility of consistently adhering to a particular course of action in similar situations. Hare (1981) argues for a rule-utilitarian approach to devising an ethical code for psychiatrists, writing:

> (psychiatrists) should consider a wide variety of particular cases and think what ought to be done in them, for the greatest good of those affected. And then they should select those principles and practises whose general acceptance would yield the closest approximation to the actions which would be done if all cases were subjected to the same leisured scrutiny (p. 38).

Thus, rule utilitarianism resolves the problems inherent in pure or 'act' utilitarianism by devising sets of rules which are in most cases likely to maximize the good if consistently obeyed.

DEONTOLOGICAL THEORIES

As opposed to utilitarian theories, deontological theories propose that there are some basic universal ethical principles which determine the morality of conduct, and actions must be judged not by their consequences but by their conformity with these basic principles which are absolute in themselves. The concept of 'rights' fits most comfortably within the deontological school of thought, with adherents of this theory asserting that there are basic human rights, such as the right to life, which may not be violated, no matter how much such violation may benefit others in the environment. Ethical conduct as conceptualized by this theory is therefore seen in terms of relationships or contracts between individuals, as one person's posession of rights implies another's responsibility to respect and protect these rights. Thus, the differences between deontological and utilitarian theories lie at a very basic level of conceptualization.

Deontological theorists believe that something other than the consequences of an action determine its morality and therefore in determining the ethicality of a behaviour do not consider how the behaviour affects all the individuals involved. There are of course, practical difficulties in the application of this theory which seem to lie in the area of solving ethical dilemmas. These problems will be discussed more fully at a later stage in this chapter, but, briefly stated, deontological theories are confounded at the point where two of the component ethical principles (which are regarded as binding and absolute) prescribe a paradox in action – i.e. if one ethical principle dictates action which is exactly opposite to the action dictated by another principle in a specific situation.

In comparing utilitarian and deontological theories the central differences in approach between the two are immediately apparent. The problems inherent in the 'pure' form of utilitarian thinking have been discussed. So, for the purposes of further discussion, let us consider merely rule utilitarianism and deontological theory. It has been seen that rule utilitarians regard adherence to sets of principles and rules as having maximal utility within a social system. Is it not possible, then, that the same principles which could arise out of an underlying deontological approach could also be derived out of a rule-utilitarian approach? Hare (1981) illustrates that this may well be so. He points out that the central principle inherent in most professional ethical codes is that the client's interests must be given priority over the claims of any other person. At face value, this is anything but a utilitarian principle, bearing in mind the basic tenet of utilitarianism that the effects of any action on *all* persons involved must be calculated before it may be regarded as ethically justifiable.

However, rule utilitarians would agree that in professional relationships the client's interest must be of paramount importance. Hare explains:

> This is because the relationship between a psychiatrist and his patient, based on mutual trust and confidentiality, has immense utility, and the destruction of this relationship is likely, except in

extreme and rare instances, to do more harm than good. So we have the paradoxical result that a utilitarian critical thinker would recommend on utilitarian grounds, the cultivation of practices which are not themselves overtly utilitarian, but appeal to such notions as the patient's rights to confidentiality (p. 39).

Using similar reasoning it appears likely that many if not all of the principles incorporated within a deontological approach to ethical decision-making could also be selected on the basis of rule-utilitarian reasoning. Thus, at this point there seem to be few practical grounds for preferring one of the theories above the other.

ETHICAL PRINCIPLES

Any number of ethical principles may be incorporated within an ethical system, but there are three widely accepted principles outlined amongst others by Ross (1930) and Beauchamp and Childress (1983) which appear to be particularly relevant to the practice of clinical psychology, all of which could be encompassed within either a deontological or rule-utilitarian basic approach. These principles are those of Autonomy, Non-maleficence and Beneficence, which will be briefly outlined here and which will provide the basis for much of the discussion in the body of this book.

AUTONOMY

Very succinctly stated, this principle asserts that individuals should be free to act according to their own beliefs and principles providing that, in doing so, they do not impede the freedom of others to do the same. This implies that at any point where an individual needs to make a decision between alternative courses of action he should be allowed to do so free of compulsion or coercion by any external agent.

An immediately apparent difficulty with the application of this principle within any human society is the conflict between attempts to preserve individual autonomy and the simultaneous necessity for laws by which governments attempt to ensure the harmonious functioning of society. Some theorists assert that these concepts of authority and autonomy are so contradictory as to be irreconcilable because the principle of autonomy dictates that individual choices should be made completely unimpeded by the influence of any authority. However, others argue that this is not necessarily so because in most democratic social systems governing bodies are autonomously chosen and therefore the decision to obey authority is itself autonomous.

For clinical psychologists, an awareness of the complex counterplay between

7

the authority they possess by virtue of their specialized knowledge and their clients' right to autonomy is essential.

Within professional relationships psychologists may unconsciously exert coercion on their clients in their eagerness to promote what they regard as the best treatment. While their motives are generally innocent, this type of coercion violates the principle of autonomy which asserts that clients must be allowed to make autonomous decisions regarding their own treatment. However, in order to make such decisions, clients must be in possession of all the relevant information pertaining to the likely outcome of a course of treatment, the nature of the involvement which would be required of them, and the availability of alternatives to the type of treatment preferred by the psychologist. It is the psychologist's duty to ensure that clients are in possession of all this information and have given full consent before they embark upon any psychological treatment. This principle of 'informed consent' safeguards the client's autonomy in the professional relationship and must be applied in all areas of the practice of clinical psychology, as will be seen in later chapters.

A difficulty with the practical application of the principle of informed consent arises when for one reason or another the client is regarded as incapable of making an autonomous decision. It is generally agreed that environmental and psychological constraints on individuals may prohibit autonomous decision-making if they are sufficient to place the individual under a significant degree of coercion or compulsion. Thus, prison and mental hospital inmates may not be autonomous agents by virtue of their coercive external environment, while the decision of a severely depressed patient to commit suicide may not be truly autonomous in nature because the psychological disability of depression may cloud the reasoning which is essential in such decisions. Naturally, the evaluation of people as unable to make autonomous decisions is difficult and open to abuse, as no clear guidelines can be established as to when or how to make such a judgement, especially where the constraints are psychological rather than tangible environmental factors. Thus, great care must be taken, both in judging individuals as non-autonomous agents and in the consequent management of such people. Normally, it is the responsibility of some other person, who has a degree of authority over the non-autonomous individual, to make the kind of decisions on behalf of the other which he presumably would have made for himself. These kinds of decisions are most accurately made in consultation with relations or others close to the individual concerned, who can give some indication as to his or her characteristic attitudes and values. In such cases, where autonomy can not be ensured, the remaining two principles of non-maleficence and beneficence must be strictly adhered to by the authority concerned, in making decisions on behalf of another.

PRINCIPLE OF NON-MALEFICENCE

The basic axiom of this principle is the directive to 'do no harm', with the definition of harm including a broad range of negative consequences from overt physical and mental suffering to injury to reputation, property and liberty. Both intentional harm and exposure of others to the risk of harm are included in this principle, with the former being totally prohibited, and the latter permissible only in special circumstances. These circumstances are those where the likelihood of a certain action producing positive consequences outweighs the degree of possible harm arising out of such action. In order to decide whether these circumstances exist, a procedure known as detriment-benefit analysis must be conducted. This involves assigning relative weightings to potential benefits and harms and is obviously an extremely difficult task, especially where benefits and harms are intangible and difficult to define such as psychological well-being or distress. The primary prerequisite here is that sufficient attention has been given to this weighting process – i.e. that 'due care' has been taken in deciding on actions with possible negative consequences. Where such care has not been taken, the practitioner responsible may be justifiably accused of violating the principle of non-maleficence through negligence.

PRINCIPLE OF BENEFICENCE

Closely related to the principle of non-maleficence, this principle asserts the duty to actively contribute to others' health and welfare by preventing harmful consequences, removing harmful conditions and positive benefiting of others.

The most important concept incorporated within this principle is that of cost-benefit analysis which is similar in principle to the detriment-benefit analysis described under the principle of non-maleficence. The underlying principle of cost-benefit analysis is that where a number of alternative courses of action are possible in a particular situation, the chosen action should be that which provides the most benefits for the lowest cost, where cost is calculated on a number of different dimensions including direct harm and investment of resources. Thus, in combining the principles of non-maleficence and beneficence, the ethical practitioner would immediately discount any action which would possibly result in more harm than good (non-maleficence) and, from the other possible courses of action, would choose the one which would maximally benefit the client while exposing him or her to minimal risk of harm or loss (beneficence). Once again, this type of analysis implies a quantifying model which is not always easy to apply. There is no easy way of measuring psychological benefits and costs and the process therefore requires a sensitive and insightful clinician working in close conjunction with the client.

THE NATURE OF RULES

The value of rules is that they provide instant guidelines as to ethical behaviour across a wide range of possible circumstances thereby relieving the practitioner of the difficult and time-consuming task of making independent ethical judgements in every new situation. Without such rules, the profession and public would need to rely upon every individual practitioner's willingness to engage in such careful consideration and upon the ability of each to view ethically complex conditions objectively and free of self-interest. However, while these are undoubted advantages to ethical rules, the nature of these rules may also raise some practical problems.

Traditionally, rules have been regarded either as 'rules of thumb' or 'absolute rules' (Beauchamp & Childress, 1983). The former are general guidelines for behaviour which may or may not be followed depending on the particular circumstances under which the practitioner is acting. Because of their expendable nature, such rules do not ensure that ethical conduct will emerge and they also provide no measure of the ethicality of an individual's conduct. In other words, in regulating a profession, no practitioner can be accused of unethical conduct for failing to obey a rule which was not binding in the first place. The alternative type of rules – that is, absolute rules – are, on the other hand, completely binding and may never be broken under any circumstances. Because of their absolute nature, such rules tend to be worded in very broad terms, such as 'be conscientious' or 'be caring', and this in itself leads to difficulties because of the problems inherent in defining precisely and accurately these general terms. Consider, for example, the difficulties in defining terms such as 'conscientiousness' and 'caring'.

If rules are to be of any use in regulating conduct it is apparent that they can be neither rules of thumb nor absolute rules because the former are too expendable, while the latter are too binding and, of necessity, too general. It is in considering the nature of ethical dilemmas that the real difficulties with the compilation of sets of rules becomes apparent, because, with such consideration, it becomes apparent that in order for an ethical code to be adequately practical and useful, the rules it incorporates need to be to some extent binding and to some extent expendable.

Ethical dilemmas arise when practitioners are confronted with situations in which two or more accepted rules come into conflict by dictating opposing courses of action. For example, the rules 'you must not betray a confidence' and 'you must not lie' come into conflict and thereby constitute an ethical dilemma when to tell the truth would be to betray a confidence. Many similar examples can be imagined and it is these kinds of relatively common situations which pose the greatest challenge in constructing ethical codes. Sieghart (1982) proposes that such conflicts are in fact the very subject matter of ethical debate,

10

writing: 'Its central field of study is how people behave when they are faced with a conflict between two or more moral principles to which they subscribe . . . without such conflicts there are no moral problems' (p. 26). He goes further to emphasize the importance of accounting for ethical dilemmas within professional ethical codes:

> Professional codes, if they are to be worth anything, cannot merely confine themselves to asserting that there is a problem and leaving it at that – let alone leaving it to individual members of the profession to solve the dilemma as best they can, consulting their unguided consciences and perhaps a few respected colleagues. At the least, such a code must say something about how to approach this kind of problem (p. 31).

Ross (1930) proposes an alternative way of conceptualizing the nature of rules which goes some way to providing a solution to the problem of ethical dilemmas. He suggests that rules be regarded neither as 'rules of thumb' nor as absolute, but as *prima facie* duties' in any particular situation. This means that while rules constitute strong moral reasons for performing particular acts, they do not necessarily prevail over other *prima facie* duties and may therefore be over-ridden under particular circumstances. This suggests that, where there is no competition between rules, the single applicable rule for a particular situation should be obeyed, but where more than one rule is applicable, some weighting process must be conducted by which it may be determined which rule has priority. Thus, Ross has partly solved the problem of conceptualizing the nature of rules, by viewing them as both binding and expendable. However, the next step is to ask how such rules or *prima facie* duties should be weighted in order to decide which should have priority.

SOLVING ETHICAL DILEMMAS

On what basis does one decide which rule should be followed where many seemingly equally important rules are all applicable? In answering this question, it is suggested that the ethical theory which underlies one's ethical decision-making procedure will be relevant. For this reason, let us briefly recap the major features of each of the two theories discussed earlier in this chapter. It was seen that the same ethical principles could theoretically be encompassed within either a rule-utilitarian or deontological approach and that therefore each theory could give rise to very similar sets of rules for particular practical situations. The major difference between the two theories is that rule-utilitarianism holds as its basic assumption only the directive to 'maximize the good', whereas rule-deontological theory asserts that the ethical principles it

11

incorporates are all absolute and inviolable and therefore presumably equal to one another in importance.

The question now arises as to whether these differences between the two theories have implications for the resolution of ethical dilemmas. Referring back to figure 1, it was seen that an ethical system may be diagrammatically represented as follows.

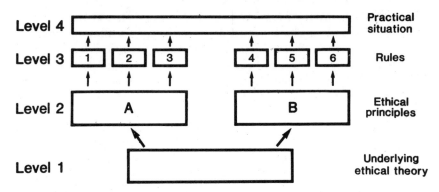

FIG. 2 : The structure underlying an Ethically Conflictual Situation

Referring to this diagram, imagine a situation in which rules 1 and 3 are in conflict – that is both are equally applicable in a particular situation. How would one go about solving the dilemma? It is suggested that one way of doing so would be to refer one level down from the level of rules – that is to the level of ethical principles. At this level it is apparent that both rules derive from the same ethical principle – in this case, principle A. In this case, then, probably the best way of assigning weightings to these rules would be to decide which of the two, in this particular situation, would best fulfil the dictates of principle A, and then to assign priority to that rule. Thus, with this kind of dilemma, the same conclusion would be reached whatever the underlying ethical theory.

Let us now consider another situation in which rules 2 and 5 are in conflict. In this case, upon referring down to the level of ethical principles, it is apparent that no solution is possible because the two rules derive from different principles – and thus the principles as well as the rules are in conflict. It is therefore necessary to refer further down the hierarchy to the level of the ethical theory in order to find some resolution. This is the point where some difference may be found between the approaches dictated by each theory, and it is important to consider carefully what these approaches might be.

If the underlying ethical theory were rule-utilitarian in nature, one would note that the basic directive of the theory is to maximize the good and, logically, one would then reconsider the rules in the light of this directive and choose to follow the rule which in this situation would maximally benefit all people involved. However, if the underlying theory were rule-deontological a different approach would be necessary because, as has been pointed out, within this theory, all principles incorporated in level 2 are binding. It would therefore be necessary to devise some kind of hierarchical ordering of the principles, such that one could say, 'in this situation principle A takes priority over principle B' and 'therefore rule 2 which is linked to principle A should be followed'. The difficulty with this is that it is conceivable that in another situation the hierarchical ordering would need to be reversed, so that principle B would take priority. A practical example of this kind of switching of hierarchies is illustrated in the following two hypothetical situations. First imagine that you are a deontological thinker and that two of your ethical principles are firstly, honesty and, secondly, loyalty to friends. Now consider the first situation: You are approached by a psychopathic killer who asks you whether your friend is at home so that he can shoot him. The principle of honesty would dictate that if you knew where your friend was you should tell the killer, but ordinary moral judgement would dictate that, in this case, loyalty to your friend should take priority and you would not tell the killer. Now imagine the second situation: Your friend has suddenly become obsessed by the idea that a particular supermarket is the source of evil and has decided to place a bomb in the store on Saturday morning. The police approach you and ask whether your friend is at home so that they can apprehend him before he commits this act. In this case, ordinary moral judgement dictates that you should assist the police and therefore honesty has taken priority over loyalty. Similar, less dramatic examples of necessary changes in the priority assigned to principles across different situations may be imagined. The point is that psychologists in their day-to-day functioning are confronted by a wide variety of situations encompassing different demands and duties and to devise a different hierarchy of rules and principles for each of these situations would be an impossible task.

On the basis of the above comparison, it seems, therefore, that the rule-utilitarian ethical theory may provide a more realistic and practical basis for the ethical decision-making process and, for this reason, it is adopted as the underlying approach for further discussion in this book. It should not be imagined that applying rule-utilitarian principles to practical ethical dilemmas is an easy task. The exact consequences of an action are rarely possible to predict, and the process by which potential positive and negative consequences are to be weighted and compared in order to maximize the good, is complicated and of necessity inexact. However, this approach does provide a practical approach to resolving ethical dilemmas and must assist in ensuring that conduct is guided, not by self-interest on the part of the practitioner, but by a genuine attempt to act in an ethically acceptable manner.

ETHICAL DECISION-MAKING

The procedure by which ethical decisions are made may be summarized as follows:

Step 1: Carefully consider the practical situation and the rules which apply. Where there is only one applicable rule, act accordingly. Where there is more than one rule, proceed to Step 2.

Step 2: Refer to the level of ethical principles, ascertain out of which principle each rule derives. Where both rules derive from the same principle, follow the rule which best fulfils the dictates of the principle in this particular situation. If the rules arise out of different ethical principles proceed to Step 3.

Step 3: Refer to the basic ethical theory of rule-utilitarianism and apply its directive to the rules. Choose to follow the rule which, in this situation, maximizes the good – i.e. that which produces the most benefit for the largest number of people involved.

DEVISING THE RULES

Discussion in this chapter has been concerned with the process by which practitioners approach ethical decision-making where a set of rules has already been clearly and adequately defined. It is apparent that the adequacy of the applicable rules will have an important effect on the efficiency of the entire decision-making process and therefore, the body of this book is concerned with the kinds of rules which should be incorporated within an ethical code for clinical psychologists. It will be remembered that rules are derived by applying ethical principles to practical situations and for this reason, following chapters will consider ethical conduct by applying the basic principles of autonomy, non-maleficence and beneficence to clinical psychologists' major areas of functioning. Difficulties with the application of these principles will be pointed out and sources of ethical dilemmas identified. Finally, the rule-utilitarian approach to ethical dilemmas as described in this chapter will be illustrated as it applies to dilemmas within each major area.

2

THE DEVELOPMENT OF CLINICAL PSYCHOLOGY AS A PROFESSION

It has been seen that guidelines for ethical behaviour in clinical psychology may be derived by applying the three ethical principles of autonomy, non-maleficence and beneficence to the practical situations in which clinical psychologists are called to make ethical decisions. The purpose of this chapter is to provide a brief outline of the major current areas of expertise of the clinical psychologist. As background to this outline, the historical development of clinical psychology, from its academic beginnings to the point where it had developed into a profession in the true sense of offering a range of valued services to the public, will be described. The growth of the professional organization of clinical psychology as it occurred in the United States of America will also be described, as will the American Psychological Association's development of an ethical code for psychologists, because it has been largely these American developments which have given impetus to the development of similar professional organizations in other Western countries.

The chapter concludes with a discussion of the ethical conflicts which arise for clinical psychologists out of the dual responsibilities the profession holds towards its clientele and the broader social system in which it operates.

THE HISTORY OF CLINICAL PSYCHOLOGY

Two major fields of study which emerged during the 19th century may be seen as forming the roots of clinical psychology as a profession. These were, firstly, the study of abnormal behaviour undertaken primarily by European physicians such as Charcot and Kraepelin and, later, by the American Lightner Witner, and, secondly, the study of individual differences in which the English scientist, Galton, was the major figure.

Research in these two fields gave rise to early interest in the possibility of

15

assessing mental handicap, with the term 'mental test' being coined in 1890 by Cattell. The following two decades saw the appearance of numerous books and articles on the study and assessment of human abilities, culminating in Binet's development of the first intelligence test in 1905, a test which constituted the first objective psychological instrument for the diagnosis of mental abnormality. This was a landmark in the history of clinical psychology as it provided the impetus for the development of numerous further tests and made the clinical psychologist a valuable staff member in institutions and clinics established to deal with problems of mental abnormality.

Until the outbreak of World War II, the role of the clinical psychologists within such institutions was largely confined to psychological testing and making recommendations on the basis of test results. Most of their work centred on problems of children and was conducted in university and community clinics (the first of which was established at the University of Pennsylvania in 1892 by Witner) and institutions for mentally retarded or delinquent children. Towards the end of the 1930s, emphasis on personality testing of adults in mental institutions began increasing, but the primary focus remained the testing of mental ability and deficiency.

The situation changed significantly with the advent of World War II, a change which Rotter (1964) attributes partly to the large-scale migration of European psychologists and psychiatrists, many of whom were psychoanalytically trained, to America. Their influence was to reduce the emphasis on intelligence testing and to increase the emphasis on tests of personality and deviant personality characteristics.

This movement was simultaneously reinforced by the large number of psychiatric war casualties, which led to greater public concern with the prevention and treatment of mental disorders. Psychologists and their testing techniques and skills proved extremely valuable in predicting susceptibility to the stresses of war in psychologically vulnerable recruits.

The number of men requiring psychiatric treatment at this time proved too large for the relatively small number of psychiatrists qualified to offer this treatment and psychologists were called upon to assist, with short training courses being established to equip them for this task. This trend persisted in the post-war years with psychologists becoming increasingly involved in working with adults with 'personality breakdowns' or problems, and official sanction for this new role was established at the 1949 Colorado Conference on the training of clinical psychologists, in which the United States Public Health Service strongly supported the training of clinical psychologists as psychotherapists. The range of employment possibilities for psychologists now expanded to include state hospitals, universities, private practice and industrial consulting firms.

Concurrent with the growth of the field of clinical psychology has been the establishment of professional organizations, particularly in the United States. In 1892, the American Psychological Association (APA) was founded, with its aim being the promotion of psychology as a science, and as early as 1917 the American Association of Clinical Psychologists was created. These two organizations remained separate until the postwar period when they amalgamated, with the latter becoming the Clinical Section of the former. At this time the APA was asked to specify standards of training and competence, and to set up boards and committees to develop criteria for and methods of assessment of clinical psychological practice. Accompanied as it was by the increasing trend of psychologists towards private practice in which they exercised a wide range of skills, this development firmly established clinical psychology as a profession in its own right.

THE ROLES AND FUNCTIONS OF CLINICAL PSYCHOLOGISTS

As is apparent from discussion in the previous section, the roles and functions of clinical psychologists have developed and diversified considerably since the beginnings of the profession in the 1890s. Clinical psychologists are currently employed in a wide variety of settings and work in collaboration with numerous other professionals such as psychiatrists, social workers and psychiatric nurses in mental institutions and community health services, teachers in schools and businessmen in industry. The functions which they are expected to perform in these varying settings may be classified as follows:

PSYCHOLOGICAL ASSESSMENT

The earliest developed field of expertise, this range of skills remains the exclusive domain of psychologists who alone are qualified to administer, interpret and make recommendations on the basis of the vast range of psychological tests which have been devised to date. The psychological assessment procedure requires highly developed interviewing and observational skills which complement the data obtained from psychological tests. The following categories of tests are most commonly administered:

a) aptitude tests which provide some indication of the client's abilities and potential in specific areas of functioning.
b) achievement tests which assess clients' success or otherwise in attaining certain expected levels of competence.
c) intelligence tests which measure overall cognitive capability.
d) personality tests, both projective and objective, indicating the existence of and relationship between particular personality traits, as well as the complex intrapsychic components underlying manifest personality.

e) specific diagnostic tests designed to elicit symptomatology of psychiatric syndromes.

PSYCHOTHERAPY

This area of functioning is generally shared by all members of the mental health professions, most notably psychiatric nurses, clinical social workers, psychiatrists and psychologists. Three major types of psychotherapy are practised today – individual therapy, group therapy, and marital and family therapy.

a) *Individual Therapy*

Originally practised only by psychiatrists, the first form of individual therapy was psychoanalysis, an activity which required considerable investments of time and money by the client. Currently, analysis or 'dynamic' therapy is also practised by other professionals, but the influence of the involvement of these others, particularly clinical psychologists, has been the development of and growing interest in other methods of treatment which are more time and money-efficient and require less rigorous training for practitioners. The most prominent of these new developments are Rogerian 'non-directive' therapy, Gestalt therapy and behaviour therapy, with the development of the latter being heavily influenced by the work of clinical psychologists who have particular training in learning theory. The aims of individual therapy may be divided into two approaches: Traditional long-term dynamic approaches claim to result in 'personality restructuring', whereas the modern, more short-term approaches have as their aim the resolution of problems in areas of current functioning.

b) *Group Therapy*

An increasingly popular method of therapy, group therapy focuses on the relief of problems through the exploration and modification of interpersonal relationship skills of the client. Interventions of therapists are primarily related to the processes within the group and the patterns of relationship occurring between group members, with the aim of assisting individual members to recognize and modify destructive patterns which they repeat in their private lives, and to cultivate constructive patterns which they observe and experience within the group. As in individual therapy, the therapist may be directive or non-directive and may employ varying techniques depending on his or her basic theoretical orientation. Groups may take many forms and have differing aims – e.g. experiential groups for essentially normal people wishing

18

to maximize their relationship potential, groups of psychiatric patients sharing and assisting one another in their experience of difficulties in adjusting to society, or professional groups within organizations wishing to improve their occupational functioning by ironing out interpersonal difficulties.

c) *Marital and Family Therapy*

Often regarded as a special form of group therapy, family therapy is based on the assumption that personal problems arise within a wider system of dysfunctional relationships and roles, the most immediate of which is the family. Essentially directive in approach, the therapist in this model removes the cause of the problem by manipulating the patterns of interaction between members of the family system. Once again, differing techniques are dictated by different theoretical schools of thought.

RESEARCH

Traditionally an important area of functioning in psychology, professional organizations such as the APA and many institutions employing clinical psychologists, such as state mental hospitals and universities, encourage clinical psychologists to engage in research as one of their major activities. Because of their numerous other responsibilities it is difficult for many practitioners to devote much time to this activity and those in private practice are hampered by a lack of facilities and equipment. For these reasons, clinical psychologists generally engage in less research than the psychologists registered in other categories. Nevertheless, with their particular training in research methodology and assessment techniques, clinical psychologists, of all mental health professionals, are probably the best equipped to engage in research into what remains an underdeveloped field of knowledge – the causation, treatment and prevention of emotional and behavioural disorders. In this rapidly expanding field, research therefore remains one of the most important functions of the modern clinical psychologist.

COMMUNITY MENTAL HEALTH PROGRAMMES

Growing awareness of the role of societal and economic circumstances in the etiology of psychiatric disturbance has led to a recent emphasis on preventative measures in the form of community mental health programmes. In this context, clinical psychologists must relinquish their traditional roles of diagnostician and therapist in a direct service relationship and must redefine themselves as operating in a consulting capacity. The important function here is to apply principles of action, diagnosis and treatment to problem

19

situations, analysing these and proposing solutions on the basis of current knowledge of common factors underlying emotional and behavioural disturbance. Rather than acting as a direct agent of change, the clinical psychologist involved in such a programme motivates and directs members of specific communities and of the broader society to effect reforms which will lessen the probability of psychiatric problems being generated.

LEGAL INVOLVEMENT

Increasingly, as clinical psychologists' expanding roles bring them into contact with a wider range of human concerns, the necessity for co-operation with the legal system, traditionally the guardian of the best interests of all members of society, increases. Clinical psychologists may be required to assist in the assessment of criminal responsibility or fitness to stand trial in criminal cases. They are also frequently assessors in compensation claims resulting out of physical or emotional injury, and in custody disputes. A third form of involvement may arise when clinical psychologists are required to give evidence in cases involving clients who are in therapy with them.

THE DEVELOPMENT OF ETHICAL CODES IN CLINICAL PSYCHOLOGY

The need for professional codes of ethics has been outlined in the Introduction. This section describes the process of development of such a code for clinical psychologists, specifically focusing on this process as it occurred in the United States of America, for the reasons stated earlier in this chapter.

The growth of the American Psychological Association has been briefly described earlier in this chapter. This is a powerful body with a large proportion of its membership (approximately thirty seven per cent according to Sundberg and Tyler, 1963) being clinical psychologists. Up until the immediate post-war period, the ethical codes devised for psychologists had been largely bound by existing codes of other professions, most notably medicine (Wolman, 1965). These codes lacked authenticity and relevance, and failed to provide adequate guidelines for psychologists, who encountered particular kinds of professional ethical problems which could not be accommodated by the ethical codes of other professions. It was for this reason that, under the direction of the United States Public Health Service, the APA undertook in 1948, to derive a code of ethics specifically for clinical psychologists.

The strength of the resulting code arises out of the method by which it was derived. The council adopted an empirical, inductive approach to the problem, inviting all of its members to submit examples of situations which they felt had ethical significance. On the basis of these examples, major problem areas were

20

defined and principles derived. The result was the booklet entitled *Ethical Standards of Psychologists,* published in 1953. The code embodied in this booklet was supported by a casebook of illustrative examples providing direction for practitioners faced with ethically problematic situations, and was greeted with widespread approval by American psychologists.

Wolman (1965) writes: 'To be effective the psychologist's code of ethics must be continually revised and brought up to date.' This is particularly true of clinical psychology in which research and practice are continually expanding the areas of functioning within which practitioners operate. The APA has accordingly continued a process of revision of their *Ethical Standards of Psychologists,* the most recent revision being adopted in 1981. During the process of these revisions, it became apparent that psychologists registered within different categories were working in differing settings and employing different methods and therefore required more specific guidelines for work within their respective fields. In 1980, after three years of research this problem was solved by the adoption of the 'Speciality Guidelines for the Delivery of Services Provided by (Clinical, School, Counselling, Industrial/Organizational) Psychologists', which serve as an adjunct to the more general standards. Enforcement of the standards embodied in the APA code is entrusted to the Committee on Scientific and Professional Conduct, which was established to assess and adjudicate claims' of malpractice by psychologists. They operate within specific procedures which guide them in deciding on the validity of claims and the punitive measures to be taken against transgressors.

CLINICAL PSYCHOLOGY AND SOCIETY

As was briefly mentioned in the Introduction, it is clear that in their professional roles clinical psychologists are bound to a dual responsibility. On the one hand, their special relationship with individual clients encompasses a duty to assign priority to the promotion of their clients' interests and welfare, while on the other hand they are bound by the laws of the broader society in which they work to avoid jeopardizing the interests of the community as a whole. The conflicts engendered by this dual responsibility and the debate concerning clinical psychologists' appropriate response to this conflict deserve further consideration.

The first type of conflict which arises out of the tension between these two responsibilities occurs when promotion and protection of an individual client's interests may jeopardize the wellbeing of one or more other individuals in the broader community.

It is possible, for example, that protecting a client from harm within the professional relationship may involve exposing other non-clients to the risk of harm. The degree of harm or risk of harm on both sides varies from situation

21

to situation, but in all cases the decision as to how to act constitutes an ethical conflict between the two duties of the psychologist.

The second type of conflict is broader and has evoked vigorous debate between clinical psychologists. This conflict concerns the nature of societal laws and the disparity between these laws and the underlying ethical principles to which clinical psychologists are committed.

It is assumed that the majority of laws in most societies are concerned with the protection of individuals within that society from harm or infringement of their basic rights – these would be laws which forbid murder, theft and other abuse to body or property. These laws are based on a common morality and coincide with the clinical psychologist's principles of autonomy, non-maleficence and beneficence. However, societal laws are decided upon and reinforced by a governing body which has an interest in protecting its own policies and security, and therefore at least some laws are directed to protection of the state – sometimes at the expense of protection of the rights of individual members of the society. Partly as a result of this, the legal system of any country is imperfect and allows for social customs or even statutory laws which infringe the autonomy and safety of at least some individuals. The degree to which this occurs depends on the socio-political system of each country, but it is safe to assume that in every country the rights and interest of some sections of the community are protected at the expense of others. Because of this situation, clinical psychologists are frequently placed in a position where they are hamstrung in relation to their clients – where the symptoms the client displays may be directly related to discriminatory or restrictive societal practices, or where to encourage autonomy in a client may be futile when the exercise of such autonomy is not sanctioned by the broader society.

The debate arising around this particular issue concerns the degree to which clinical psychologists should become involved in instituting social reform by actively opposing societal practices which threaten the autonomy, safety and therefore mental-health of their clients. Opinion is split between those who feel that psychologists should concern themselves only with the mental health of individual clients and others who maintain that part of the responsibility of the psychologist is to promote the mental health of all members of society and psychologists must therefore accept a degree of involvement in broader social reform.

The first school of psychologists who hold that one's role encompasses only responsibility towards individual clients hold that in dealing with clients one should be 'value-neutral'. That is, in order to foster the client's autonomy, the psychologist must not dictate to the client what the 'good' is, but allow the client to discover for himself what is 'good'. They argue that the client may only do this in a relationship with a clinical psychologist who is 'politically neutral'; any public stance on social issues on the part of the psychologist may subtly coerce the client into accepting the therapist's value judgements, thus violating the principle of autonomy. They argue further that the role-definition of a clinical psychologist does not encompass that of social or political activist, and that this role is more appropriately performed by sociologists or politicians. Bugental (1971) states that, in any case, methods of treatment which espouse humanistic values such as autonomy and responsibility automatically foster in clients a concern with broader societal issues and, furthermore, provide clients with the ability to tackle these issues and themselves become involved in social reform.

The opposing argument is that the profession of clinical psychology is established and maintained by the society within which it operates and that therefore this society to a certain extent determines the framework of the profession's functions. For example, it is argued that the diagnosis of mental illness is made with reference to societal norms, with deviance being defined in terms of an inability or unwillingness to comply with these norms. The 'curing' of mental illness therefore implies helping people to adapt to and accept social practices rather than to challenge them. The emphasis on the individual patient, advocated by psychologists who oppose active involvement in societal reform, is regarded as socially conservative, because 'it trains the individual in continuing introspection and in the interpretation of people, processes and events by methods associated with investigation of the unconscious and away from the social causes of self-defeating behaviour' (p. 235) thereby 'making personal problems of political issues' (Hurvitz, 1973, p. 233). Therefore, these writers argue that by working within the framework defined for the profession by society – that is concentrating on the individual rather than also taking cognizance of the social forces acting upon him or her – clinical psychology 'accepts the society which established it and by enabling the society to maintain itself, perpetuates the problems it was planned to abolish' (Statman, 1970, p. 15). Halleck (1971) therefore rejects the claim that psychologists should be politically neutral, arguing that such a position is impossible because 'By reinforcing the positions of those who hold power the psychiatrist (or psychologist) is committing a political act, whether he intends to or not' (p. 32).

If clinical psychologists are, in one way or another, inevitably politically involved, it is argued that they have a responsibility to actively contribute towards changing societal conditions which are not conducive to mental health, both by treatment of individual clients which encourages them to examine and confront their environment, and by confronting those societal institutions which are oppressive and restrict the autonomous functioning of individuals. It is possible that, of all members of society, clinical psychologists and other mental health professionals have a special responsibility in this regard by

23

virtue of their specialized knowledge of the societal determinants of psychological distress.

As yet there is no consensus on this issue which appears to be related to the role-definition of clinical psychologists, and is thus an issue of professional policy. It is possible that through a process of evolution of clinical psychologists' conceptualization of themselves as professionals in relation to society, some clearer stance may be adopted as to whether the pyschologist's accepted role should encompass a degree of involvement in social reform. Until such time this must remain a contentious issue.

Despite this continuing debate, there is no doubt or disagreement about the fact that clinical psychologists in performing their professional role must take cognizance of the demands and restrictions placed upon them by the broader society. It seems that there are occasions on which promotion of the client's welfare is challenged and must be tempered with the professional's responsibility towards society and occasions on which the opposite must occur. An example of the former would be if the clinical psychologist was aware that a client held strong political beliefs which made him decide to place a bomb in a crowded supermarket. The threat to innocent lives posed by this decision might make the psychologist forfeit his responsibility to protect his client for his societal responsibility to the potential victims. An example of the latter type of situation may be illustrated by the frequently quoted case of a psychologist employed by the United States Defence Force to assess the psychological suitability of soldiers to return to the battlefield after suffering psychological disturbance during the Vietnam war. The psychologist refused to participate in this assessment procedure on the grounds that it violated the ethical principles of autonomy and non-maleficence – the men he was assessing were not voluntarily involved in the war and did not wish to return to the battlefield, and recommending that they return would expose them to immense risks of physical harm. In addition, he felt that the war itself was related to the ideals of the current government, rather than to the direct interests of American society and that refusing to participate in the assessment procedure would not directly endanger the safety of the American public. In other words, this psychologist asserted that the protective function the psychologist must serve towards other members of society by, for example, preventing violent action of a client, does not extend to protection of the state or its institutions. It may be, then, that where there is no direct threat of violence or danger to society members, the psychologist is under no obligation to support the government, where such support may violate the psychologist's ethical principles by making him an agent of the state rather than of the client.

It is obvious that reconciling the two separate duties towards client and society is fraught with potential pitfalls and requires extensive care in making decisions as to ethical courses of action in many different situations. The second section of this book deals with the nature of these conflicts in more detail and makes suggestions as to ways in which they may be resolved with minimal compromise of the ethical principles which clinical pyschologists must uphold in the practice of their profession.

PART TWO

APPLIED ETHICS IN CLINICAL PSYCHOLOGY

The previous section of this book dealt with the philosophical basis of the study of ethics and the major areas of functioning of clinical psychologists which require ethical regulation. Three guiding ethical principles – those of autonomy, non-maleficence and beneficence – were identified as being of primary importance to the ethical practice of clinical psychology, and the rule-utilitarian ethical theory was proposed as a means of approaching and solving ethical dilemmas.

This section examines in more detail the application of ethical principles to the practice of clinical psychology in its various forms. Four major areas of functioning have been identified, being those of psychotherapy, psychological assessment, research and legal involvement. A further chapter examines the ethical principles in relation to professional conduct. Within each of these areas, possible sources of ethical dilemmas are identified and suggested means of resolving such dilemmas are proposed.

The final chapter in this section focuses specifically on the South African context and identifies characteristics and practices particular to this country which may introduce further complications in ethical practice for the South African clinical psychologist.

3

ETHICS IN PSYCHOTHERAPY

The ethical practice of psychotherapy has been widely debated in the professional literature. Opinions as to the appropriate roles and ethical responsibilities of psychotherapists differ not only between differing theoretical schools of psychotherapy but also between individual practitioners within each school. The purpose of this chapter is not to propose a resolution of these differences of opinion, but to outline the broadly agreed-upon areas of responsibility of psychotherapists and to examine arguments put forward by various theorists within each of these areas. The major focus of discussion will be the application of the ethical principles of autonomy, non-maleficence and beneficence to each of the areas of responsibility, with the aim of identifying ethical behaviour within each area. Commonly encountered ethical dilemmas within each area will also be examined in some detail and suggestions for resolving these will be discussed.

The major areas in which ethical dilemmas are encountered in psychotherapy are identified in this chapter as being: values and goals in psychotherapy; the therapist's responsibilities towards clients; and methods and techniques of psychotherapy.

VALUES IN PSYCHOTHERAPY

The issue of the psychotherapist's values and the effects that these have on the process of psychotherapy is one which is frequently considered in the literature. Many practitioners (e.g. Breggin, 1971; Engelhardt, 1973; Kennedy, 1973; Strupp, 1980 and Will, 1981) argue that the most important guiding principle is autonomy, which implies that the therapist's obligation is to ensure that, through the exploration and understanding of the client's past and present conflicts, the client will eventually arrive at a position where he can select for himself the values by which he wishes to conduct his life. The 'personal freedom' of clients to make their own choices regarding values and to choose values which may be different from those of the therapist is therefore held to be essential. Even therapeutic models which concentrate on 'symptom-removal' rather than exploration of intrapsychic factors, maintain that they are upholding the principle of autonomy in that they are removing symptoms which impair the client's ability to function autonomously.

The therapeutic values regarded as essential within this framework have been summarized by Strupp (1980) as follows:

1. People have the right to personal freedom and independence.
2. They have rights and privileges but they also have responsibilities towards others.
3. People should be responsible for conducting their own lives without undue dependence on others.
4. People are responsible for their actions but not their feelings, fantasies, etc.
5. People's individuality should be fully respected and they should not be controlled, dominated, manipulated, coerced or indoctrinated.
6. People are entitled to make their own mistakes and to learn from their life experiences (pp. 397–398).

Will (1981) expands on these, emphasizing the autonomy of the individual client within the therapeutic relationship as well in his outside life, writing: 'The patient's freedom is a matter of great concern. He is to have freedom of choice about the form of therapy, the selection of therapist, and his ways of expressing himself within the limits of safety, public acceptance, and the necessity to preserve the treatment process itself; he is free to live in ways that may not be congenial to the therapist' (p. 209).

Strupp (1980) expresses the basic tenet of this group of practitioners thus '. . . what is unique about the enterprise of psychotherapy is the basic belief that . . . people will search for and find their own solutions to basic life problems' (p. 400).

Although the attitude suggested by the above authors may be the ideal approach, several writers have questioned the possibility of its practical application. Weisskopf-Joelson (1980) questions the possibility of the therapist maintaining a value-free neutrality in therapy, writing: 'values are bound to be disseminated during the therapeutic process regardless of the therapist's intentions. The therapist's appearance and clothing as well as the appearance of his/her office communicate values. Even a noncommittal "mmm" or a Rogerian reflection might, by its timing, suggest to the client what the therapist values as important' (p. 462). Even the process of diagnosis, theoretically based on objectively observed symptomatology, appears to be heavily influenced by the therapist's own values. Research conducted by Braginsky and Braginsky (1973) showed that when dummy 'patients' expressed political views which differed radically from those of the therapist they were judged as far more disturbed than patients who presented with the same symptoms, but expressed political views consistent with the therapist's.

Further, this 'worsening' of pathology was also noted when patients made critical rather than flattering comments about mental health professionals.

There has been some empirical evidence to support the notion that therapists' values are communicated to the client during therapy and that this has some influence on value changes in the client. Beutler (1979) quotes several research studies, including his own, which have revealed three relevant facts:

1. patients tend to evaluate the success of therapy on the basis of the therapist's initial goals rather than their own.
2. they acquire the interest patterns of their therapist, and
3. patients acquire their own therapist's values while concomitantly moving away from the value patterns of other similarly trained therapists.

It would appear from this that, while consciously attempting to avoid imposing their values on clients, therapists are unconsciously communicating their own values and reinforcing clients for adopting these values.

THE TRANSLATION OF VALUES INTO THERAPEUTIC GOALS

In the light of the seemingly inevitable transmission of the therapist's values during the course of therapy, several authors have recommended that the therapist abandon any pretence at a 'value-free' therapeutic attitude and consciously guide their clients in the direction of 'good' behaviour. A commonly accepted definition of what 'the good' would constitute here is that of Lederer (1971) who states: '"good" is that which, in the overall, and in the long run, furthers the survival of the human community' (p. 83). Statements made by these therapists include those of Smith and Petersen (1977): 'We need to guard against emphasizing individual autonomy at the expense of the community' (p. 316); Graham (1980): 'I do not think we ever convince our patients that we are neutral observers or that we are devoid of moral judgement. I think a patient can and must be informed at times that his/her behaviour is odious' (p. 371) and Garfield (1974): 'the therapist has to make a decision that he can not only "help" the client, that is, move towards the client's goal, but also that the goal is a "desirable" one' (p. 202). These writers therefore argue that, as the admirable intention to maintain the client's ultimate autonomy and freedom of choice as the sole therapeutic goal is demonstrably unattainable, the therapist then has an obligation to at least uphold the other ethical principles of non-maleficence and beneficence. That is, the therapist's goals in therapy should be to ultimately benefit the client and the broader society.

The problem with this approach is that it takes for granted the client's lack of autonomy and puts the decision as to the goals of therapy firmly into the hands of the therapist. Will (1981) emphasizes that at least in deciding on

31

what ultimate benefits should be derived from therapy, the client should be able to make an autonomous choice. He thus reinforces the view that in deciding on the goals of therapy the major decisions should be made by the client. Karasu (1980) concurs with this view and criticizes what he refers to as 'one of the most prominent negative effects in the traditional therapeutic relationship: its insufficient regard for the patient's intentionality or will' (p. 1503).

A significant ethical conflict may therefore arise, then, where the therapist's conceptualization of a desirable goal differs from the client's desired goals in therapy. It has been shown that no matter how much the therapist attempts to conceal his values and goals these are implicitly communicated to the client and, in the course of therapy, the client will be unconsciously and covertly 'persuaded' to adopt these values and goals. A possible solution to this inadvertent violation of the principle of autonomy may be for the therapist to apply the principle of informed consent during contracting with the patient for a course of therapy. This principle has been briefly discussed in chapter one and its use in relation to contracting for therapy has been supported by many authors (e.g. Ayllon and Skuban, 1973; Bastiansen, 1974; Sadoff, 1974; Schwitzgebel, 1975; Strupp, 1975; Coyne, 1976; Noll, 1976; Robitscher, 1978; Coyne and Widiger, 1978; Hare-Mustin, 1979).

How this principle of informed consent would be applied in contracting for therapy may proceed as follows: The therapist should initially point out to the client what he perceives as desirable goals of the therapeutic process, that is he should make his own values explicit to the client. If these goals differ from the goals of the client, the client will then be able to make an autonomous choice as to whether to accept the therapist's goals or reject them, choosing instead not to engage in therapy or to attempt to find another therapist who would be prepared to work within the client's framework of values. A hypothetical example may illustrate this more clearly: A woman who feels depressed and dissatisfied with her life due to pressures on her to conform to the traditional societal role assigned to women, which involves confining her energies to housekeeping and mothering duties, consults a therapist with the specific aim of being able to accept this role without being depressed. In other words, the woman is saying to the therapist that she values the traditional woman's role and wishes to maintain her current functioning within this role, but does want her depression removed – her goal is adaptation to the role rather than questioning of it. The therapist she consults may, on the other hand, feel that his ethical principles of autonomy and beneficence dictate a different therapeutic goal. He may feel that the client will derive more benefit from a critical examination of the pressures to conform to such a role, and the alternatives which are available to her, after which she will be able to make an autonomous choice as to her future actions. There is therefore a conflict between the client's goal of ultimate adaptation and the therapist's desired goal of ultimate autonomy. The therapist's duty in such a case would be to make explicit his standpoint – in other words, to tell the woman that he personally values autonomy rather than adaptation and that his goal for therapy would be to work towards such autonomy. The woman could then decide for herself whether to continue in therapy or to preserve her original goal and not risk the threat to ultimate adaptation that therapy may represent.

A similar difficult situation arises when the therapist realizes that the agreed-upon goal of therapy may require the client to sacrifice other aspects of his or her life which are valued in themselves. A well-known case reported by Cohen and Smith (1976) and discussed at some length in the literature (e.g. Coyne, 1976; McLemore and Court, 1977) provides a good example of this kind of situation. In this case, the therapists felt that the cause of the patient's subjective distress and obsessional symptoms was the restrictions imposed on her by virtue of her religious affiliation. Therapeutic outcome was regarded as successful, but involved some challenging of the client's religious beliefs which eventuated in her renunciation of her religion. (This outcome had been predicted by the therapists but never made explicit to the client.) As a result of this, her marriage became conflicted, in that her husband remained staunchly religious, and she eventually obtained a divorce. The issue here was that the client, on entering therapy, had no intention of changing her religion or of obtaining a divorce and was not aware that working towards her goal of relief from distress would possibly involve these losses. Had she been aware of this possibility, she may well have decided not to engage in therapy. Such indirect effects of therapy are frequently anticipated by psychotherapists and the question arises as to whether a client's decision to begin therapy can be fully autonomous unless he or she is aware of the possibility of these effects and can weigh the benefits of achieving the therapeutic goal against the possible losses which may be involved. This weighting should arguably not be the therapist's task as he can never be fully aware of the value which the client assigns to the various factors involved.

Again, it seems that the principle of informed consent should be applied. (Hare-Mustin et al, 1979; Coyne and Widiger, 1978.) Where the therapist is aware that 'successful' therapeutic outcome, in terms of reaching the agreed-upon goal, may involve the loss or alteration of currently valued circumstances and beliefs of the client, this must be made explicit to the client before therapy is begun. If the value the client assigns to the threatened relationships or beliefs outweighs the potential benefits he feels he will gain from achieving a specific goal, he may well choose not to engage in therapy. Failure to inform clients of these aspects may be seen as 'tricking' the client where previously held values are challenged and changed. Where the client has no objections to having his values challenged this does not represent a problem, but the principle of autonomy dictates that the choice must be the client's and not the therapist's.

Of course, it frequently occurs during the process of therapy that either therapist or client may perceive the possibility of changing the originally agreed-upon goals. At this point, the changes in perception must be discussed and new goals negotiated in a similar fashion.

RESPONSIBILITIES TOWARDS THE CLIENT

There is considerable agreement in the literature as to the range of responsibilities which the therapist incurs in relation to the client. These responsibilities can be seen as concerning issues of confidentiality, competence, dual relationships with clients, and involuntary hospitalization and the right to treatment. The nature of these responsibilities and their ethical justification in terms of the principles of autonomy, non-maleficence, beneficence and justice will be discussed. Despite general agreement as to the nature of these responsibilities there are arguments within the literature as to the specific ways in which these responsibilities are realized within practical situations. These arguments will also be presented in this section. Finally, proposals will be made as to how ethical dilemmas which arise in relation to these responsibilities may be approached.

CONFIDENTIALITY

Numerous authors have discussed the issue of confidentiality in psychotherapy (Dubey, 1974; Plaut, 1974; Lowental, 1974; Teichner, 1975; Denkowski and Denkowski, 1982; Mariner, 1967). The rationale for the ensuring of therapeutic confidentiality is based on the principles of autonomy (the client should be able to choose which information he wishes to reveal to which persons); beneficence (the client will be unable to reap the full benefits of therapy without a trusting relationship with the therapist); and non-maleficence (the client may be harmed by the release of private information to other sources). Denkowski and Denkowski (1982) question the necessity for absolute confidentiality in non-psychoanalytic therapy, but still maintain that in order to protect patients from potential harm, it is in general essential to respect confidentiality.

Several factors, especially in the United States, are making the maintenance of confidentiality increasingly problematic for therapists. The major difficulties appear to derive from the increased subsidization of therapy fees by third parties such as medical aid associations, the increasing use of computer storage for confidential material, the nature of therapeutic work in institutions or mental health agencies and several recent legal rulings which appear to reduce

34

the patient's rights to confidentiality and emphasize the demands on the therapist to breach confidentiality in certain circumstances.

Insurance companies in the United States who are increasingly bearing the financial burden of many clients' therapy payments are naturally concerned about the nature and effectiveness of the services for which they are paying and this has led to their increasing demands on therapists for information regarding the diagnosis, treatment plans and therapeutic progress of individual clients. Many therapists are concerned about the release of this information to such bodies particularly where the client's employer may also have access to it.

Increasingly, large institutions and therapeutic agencies are making use of computer storage systems for confidential data. While this facilitates the efficient organization of the institution, it also provides easier access to confidential information by many potentially interested parties. There is special concern over the fact that many government agencies can gain access to such information by putting their own computers directly on-line to an institution's system and, through this so-called 'computer rape' obtain confidential data without the institution's knowledge. Therapists are therefore encouraged to carefully monitor the nature of the information programmed into such systems, maintaining it at a minimum level.

Demands on the therapist working within such an institution are also frequently not conducive to maintenance of confidentiality. The sharing of information with other members of a therapeutic team via case conferences immediately diffuses the responsibility to maintain confidentiality and the release of information therefore becomes more difficult to maintain and control. In addition, the established tradition of 'co-operation between agencies' means that therapists within such institutions are frequently requested to reveal information to other agencies who have some interest in the client. Dubey (1974) argues that this policy deprives the client of the right to confidentiality and, particularly where the client refuses to release such information, the therapist should run the risk of being labelled 'unco-operative' by his employing institution and also refuse to divulge such data. He argues that despite the potential extra expense, such other agencies should employ their own independent psychologists to evaluate the particular aspects of the client in which they are interested, pointing out that, as soon as information is released by an individual therapist to a third party, the therapist loses control over the further dissemination of this data and the client's rights may be more easily further eroded.

The major recent area of concern has been the legal injunction on therapists to breach confidentiality when the client is perceived to be dangerous to himself or others. Here, 'dangerousness' has not been clearly defined and appears to encompass any form of criminal act. Robinson (1974) has argued against this broad definition and recommended that the concept of dangerousness be limited to private harm as in many societies activities which do not involve private harm, such as political activism, are also frequently defined as criminal acts. Further discussion of the implications of these legal rulings may be found in chapter eight.

At this point it is important to note that the privilege of confidentiality is considered to be the client's privilege and not the therapist's, and therefore if the client gives consent for the release of certain kinds of information, the therapist is generally regarded as being obliged to comply in revealing the information. Dubey (1974) presents several arguments for making the privilege of therapeutic confidentiality the therapist's as well as the client's.

Firstly, clients are frequently unaware of the possible consequences of giving consent for the release of confidential information and may be unwittingly compromising their position by so doing in certain circumstances.

Secondly, in some situations clients may be coerced into giving this consent. For example, in applying for employment, clients are frequently asked whether they are or have been in therapy. If they are honest and reply affirmatively to this question they are then asked to give permission for the potential employer to contact the therapist and ask questions about the client's condition and progress. If the client were to refuse to grant this permission his application would undoubtedly be jeopardised and he therefore has little choice but to consent.

Finally, in cases where the revealing of confidential therapeutic information would benefit the client in some way (for example, in gaining exemption from military service), Dubey argues that the therapist's compliance in supplying the information reinforces the secondary gain which the client derives from his symtomatology. This situation would be antithetical to the goals of the therapeutic process.

Thus, Dubey argues for a form of absolute confidentiality in which the therapist refuses to reveal confidential information about the client to any third party no matter what the purposes of the request for information and regardless of whether the client has given consent or not. Obviously where the therapist is required by law to reveal such information a dilemma arises, but Dubey suggests that all agencies which commonly request such information from therapists, including the courts, should employ independent professionals who are trained in eliciting the kind of information which the agency requires. He maintains that wherever possible, the therapeutic treatment of the client and evaluation of the client for other purposes should be separate tasks performed by separate professionals.

Laudable as this suggestion may be in maximizing the welfare of the client, many practical problems may be encountered in its implementation, including wastage of both time and money resources, and it therefore seems unlikely that such a system will be implemented in the near future. Psychotherapists will therefore continue to be faced with many conflicts over the issue of confidentiality for some time to come.

Possibly the rule-utilitarian approach to ethical dilemmas may be useful here. It seems that when deciding whether or not to breach confidentiality in the kinds of situations discussed in this section, the potential costs and benefits for all people involved need to be considered. Take, for example, a situation where a client asks his therapist to compile a report requested by a potential employer. In cases where the information revealed by the therapist would constitute solid support of the client's application, a dilemma may arise. Do the benefits of maintaining therapeutic confidentiality outweigh the benefits to the client in gaining the employment he desires? It seems that the answer to this question will lie in the importance to the client of the employment prospect and the importance the potential employer will ascribe to the therapist's report. Where the therapist's report will make the essential difference to whether the client is employed or not, and where the client has been unemployed for some time or urgently needs the remuneration from the job, the therapist may well decide that the benefits for the client inherent in writing the report outweigh the benefits of absolute confidentiality. In other circumstances, of course, the therapist may decide that the client will not benefit from such a report or that the benefits would not be sufficient to outweigh the advantages of confidentiality, and would therefore refuse the client's request.

In any circumstances, the principle of informed consent dictates that if the therapist is aware that confidentiality of the therapy sessions cannot be absolute, the client must be informed of the limits of confidentiality and, as far as he is aware, the therapist must explain to the client who else has access to the private information as well as the use to which such information will be put. If the client has been asked, for example by a potential employer, to consent to a request for a report from the therapist, the therapist must explain what the consequences of giving such consent may be, and should also discuss with the client the interpretations the third party may make of his refusing such consent.

COMPETENCE

Clients who consult psychotherapists do so with the expectation that the therapist will be able to assist them in resolving their difficulties. The principles of non-maleficence and beneficence dictate that, in undertaking psychotherapy with a client, the therapist will possess the necessary competence to perform services which will not harm the client and which will have some beneficial result. Clients are frequently poorly informed as to the competence of therapists, and the therapists themselves and their professional

37

organizations must be responsible for ensuring professional standards of practice. Several factors appear to be important in assessing and maintaining the competence of clinical psychologists as psychotherapists.

a) *Basic Training and Professional Qualifications*

Most countries have an agreed upon set of academic qualifications without which the potential clinical psychologist may not become registered and may therefore not practise psychotherapy. Due to the relatively short time period of these basic training courses, frequently they provide only a broad introduction to the various modes and models of psychotherapy or else emphasize the practise of only one model, while affording other models only a cursory examination or neglecting them completely. In addition, it could be argued that it is only through experience in psychotherapy that an adequate level of competence is eventually attained. It is doubtful that there is sufficient time during the duration of the basic training course to gain enough experience to achieve this level. Therefore, although psychologists are theoretically academically qualified to engage in any model of psychotherapy of their choice upon graduation from such a training course, their competence is of necessity initially limited due to their limited exposure to both the theoretical and practical aspects of many of these models. The differences between training programmes at differing universities both in terms of the focus and the intensity of training in psychotherapy produces extra complications in that psychologists who initially embark on careers as psychotherapists do not have a standardized minimal level of competence in any aspects of psychotherapy. Although it would not be practical or even desirable to standardize the main focus or preferred models of all psychotherapeutic training programmes, it may be helpful to set certain basic minimal standards for these programmes so that the public may be assured of some basic level of competence in novice therapists.

In order to achieve the desired level of competence in psychotherapy with the minimum risk of harm to clients it appears necessary then to advocate some post-graduate in-practice training for newly graduated therapists in the form of advanced training programmes in particular models and techniques and/or regular required supervision by more experienced practitioners for a stipulated time period.

Hare-Mustin et al (1979) write that clients are usually uncertain about the specialities and training of various professionals. An example is the frequently mistaken understanding of the training and qualifications of clinical psychologists as opposed to psychiatrists. They suggest that a short description of the qualifications and relevant experience of the therapist may help to dispel clients' unrealistic expectations.

It is particularly important for therapists-in-training to inform clients of this fact, with the reassurance that they are under the supervision of a qualified and experienced therapist. Robitscher (1978) acknowledges the danger of this information operating in the service of the resistance of the client, thus impeding therapeutic progress to a certain extent, but nevertheless maintains that the client's right to choose his therapist on an informed basis outweighs the potential negative effects of imparting such information.

b) *Continuing Training and the Maintenance of Competence*

Singer (1980) points out that: 'Psychotherapy is best understood as an application of available scientific knowledge' (p. 372). Because 'available scientific knowledge' is constantly expanding and revealing new facts and relationships between facts, Singer asserts that in order to maintain an optimum level of competence, psychotherapists must regularly scan scientific journals in order to modify both their theoretical understanding and practical applications of psychotherapeutic methods in order to benefit their clients maximally.

It could be argued that to adhere tenaciously to one model of therapy and apply it in the treatment of all clients, even where it is obviously not maximally beneficial, may constitute incompetence in psychotherapists. In such cases, therapists must be prepared to refer such clients to more appropriate sources of help, or remain alert to the possibilities of other methods, especially those newly developed, which may be of more benefit. Continuing training and education in such new techniques and methods even for experienced therapists would then be desirable to ensure competence. This aspect will be discussed further in the section on methods and techniques in psychotherapy. In any event, it remains essential for therapists to be aware of new developments and discoveries within their preferred model and not to assume that their basic training and years of experience make them sufficiently competent to continue practising within that model.

c) *Personal needs of the Therapist*

Conflicts and problems within the therapist himself frequently interfere with the competent delivery of psychotherapeutic services. Such difficulties may obscure the therapist's understanding of the client's situation and may also lead him into using the process of psychotherapy to fulfil his own needs. In his discussion of the major causes of unethical practice, Schwebel (1955) identifies the therapist's self-interest as one of the major factors to be considered. He lists three main types of self-interest:

39

1. Personal profit motive – clients may be engaged inappropriately or the therapeutic process itself artificially prolonged because of the therapist's reliance on a regular clientele for his livelihood.
2. Need for self enchancement – inappropriate dependence in clients may be fostered as a means of validating the therapist's conceptualization of himself as an expert and helpful person.
3. Need to maintain security and status – the limitations of the therapeutic relationship and the possible failure of the therapeutic endeavour may not be recognized by the therapist who needs his role as therapist to gain social status and security.

Brown (1980) in his discussion of the various forms of usuriousness in psychotherapy, agrees with the points raised by Schwebel and in addition mentions 'those instances wherein the patient is used to continue to work out the therapist's personal dynamics in relationship' (p. 422). The therapist needs to be constantly aware of the possibility of such personal problems and needs interfering in the psychotherapeutic process, and where he has identified such difficulties should consult with peers, or a supervisor, and if necessary, enter therapy himself in order to resolve these problems.

d) *Recognition of Limitations*

Although clients frequently feel that therapy will be the panacea for all their problems, it is widely recognized that all therapeutic models and methods have limited effectiveness. It is the therapist's responsibility to recognize these limitations and, where therapy is no longer beneficial to the client, to terminate the process and refer the client to alternative sources of help.

Apart from these technical limitations, the therapist's personal limitations need to be considered. Some of these were considered in the previous section, but, in addition, many therapists find that because of personal factors, they prefer working with some clients and find it very difficult to work with others. As the therapist's personal feelings towards the client undoubtedly affect his competence in offering adequate therapy, these types of personal limitations also need to be recognized. Many personal needs of therapists obscure their recognition of limitations, whether technical or personal, and this must be detrimental to clients who are consequently denied the opportunity for more successful treatment elsewhere. This situation is aggravated by the fact that the more inexperienced a therapist is, the more inadequate and insecure he feels in his role and consequently the less willing he is to admit to these kinds of limitations. This means that the more incompetent therapists are in fact the least likely to recognize their limitations, and highlights the need for monitoring through supervision, especially for novice therapists.

In summary, the ethical psychotherapist ensures his competence by ongoing training and supervision, caution in the practise of new or unfamiliar methods and recognition of technical and personal factors which limit his competence with particular clients. He consciously attempts to resolve these latter limitations by adequate supervision or by himself entering psychotherapy.

DUAL RELATIONSHIPS WITH CLIENTS

The APA ethical code outlines the responsibility of psychotherapists to avoid engaging in dual relationships with clients which could be detrimental, specifically identifying sexual relationships with clients as unethical. It is primarily the principle of non-maleficence from which these injunctions appear to be derived. This section will look at the theoretical and ethical arguments against such dual relationships, firstly in general and then specifically with regard to sexual relationships. Some suggestions for ameliorating the negative effects of dual relationships other than sexual ones (which are always ill advised) will also be considered.

Roll and Millen (1981) discuss the negative effects of dual relationships with clients, where the client is a friend or acquaintance of the therapist. They identify the following negative effects:

1. *Loss of the friendship* – Because of the particular restrictions and roles inherent in the practice of psychotherapy, new stresses are introduced into the relationship which may lead to the end of the friendship.
2. *Complication of the transference* – The client who knows the therapist in another context will experience difficulties in establishing a therapeutic transference relationship. Interpretation of transference will also be more complicated in that the therapist cannot be sure whether the client's reactions to him are based in the therapeutic relationship or on the client's perception of him outside the relationship. This increases the complexity of an already difficult aspect of therapy and may impede the client's therapeutic progress.
3. *Support of grandiosity* – The inevitable disequilibrium of power and the relative powerfulness of the therapist may well extend back into the previously established relationship and, should the therapist be susceptible to this kind of inflation of his role, his professional competence and standards in general may be eroded.

Despite these contra-indications, Roll and Millin (1981) recognize that in some cases, particularly in relatively small communities, the therapist will not be able to avoid treating some clients with whom they also have some extra-therapeutic contact. The client may be a friend, a student or even a professional such as the doctor or dentist of the therapist. Applying the rule-utilitarian approach, what the therapist would need to consider in such cases may include the need of the client for his help, the possibility of obtaining comparable help from other sources, the extent of the damage to the previous relationship which could arise from therapy and the extent to which the therapist feels he is competent to deal with the complications which may arise out of such a therapeutic relationship. Where the client is in dire need of help and the therapist is the only available source, the benefits of treatment may well outweigh the possible harm and the rule-utilitarian approach would dictate that the therapy should be attempted. In fact, it may well be unethical in some such cases to refuse to treat the client. In the light of this, Roll and Millin provide some guidelines which minimize the potential negative effects in dealing with such cases.

1. *Don't do it* – It is re-emphasized that, wherever possible, such relationships should be avoided by referring acquaintances to professional colleagues or alternative sources of help.
2. *The transference relationship is real and the 'real' relationship is real* – Two temptations may arise in these cases. One is to treat all reactions of the acquaintance-client as transference and the other is to ignore the transference and concentrate on the real relationship. Therapists are advised to discuss the problems of the dual relationship with the client early in therapy, and to continue to interpret the transference. Failure to do so may contaminate the extra-therapeutic relationship with the unresolved transference reactions of the client.
3. *Corollary to above: get supervision or consultation.* Supervision is an aid to distinguishing transference and countertransference reactions from the transactions which derive out of the original relationship.
4. *Rigidify.* The negative effects of overlap between the therapeutic relationship and outside relationship may be minimized by more than usually strict adherence to the limits of therapy (especially time limits) and by specifically requesting that issues raised in therapy not be carried over to the outside context.
5. *Organize a hierarchy of values* – Some decision about the relative importance and dominance of each relationship appears to be necessary. Because special obligations are incurred by the therapist towards the client which are qualitatively different from those in relationships with friends and acquaintances, it is suggested that the therapeutic relationship should always be given priority as long as the dual relationship continues.
6. *Be prepared to lose the friendship* – Not only must the therapist be prepared to lose the friendship of his client in the interests of therapeutic progress, but where the client is a relation or a close friend of a friend of the therapist, the therapist must be prepared to forfeit this friendship as well.

Where he is not prepared to lose the friendship, the therapeutic endeavour should not be undertaken.

7. *Avoid discussing case material* – This advice seems to apply not only when the client is a friend, but also where there is the danger that the people to whom the material is being presented may be friends or relations of the client.

8. *Know when to stop* – Because of the increased danger of the therapeutic relationship with an acquaintance becoming complicated and possibly even pathological, the therapist should be more than usually alert to signs that therapy is becoming destructive so that the therapy may be terminated and the client referred.

9. *Be gratified* – The danger of gratifying personal needs through therapy with a client who is also a friend, is greatly increased. The therapist must be especially sensitive to this possibility and take active steps to ensure that his own life is sufficiently gratifying.

Roll and Millin confined their discussion to therapy with clients with whom the therapist has an already established relationship, but the establishment of friendships or other extra-therapeutic relationships with clients already in therapy is always regarded as anti-therapeutic. By far the largest proportion of writings in this area are devoted to the negative effects of sexual relationships established during the process of therapy with clients (e.g. Kardener, 1974; Hare-Mustin, 1974; Finney, 1975; Stone, 1976; Davidson, 1977; Barnhouse, 1978; Hays, 1980; Serban, 1981).

Barnhouse (1978) presents a primarily theoretical argument against therapist-client sex, arguing that, particularly in psychodynamic therapy, it is detrimental to the client for three major reasons. Firstly, within the transference relationship the client almost invariably enters into a type of parent-child relationship with the therapist and therapist-client sex can therefore be seen as having incestuous overtones. Particularly where Oedipal problems are involved, this metaphorical violation of the incest taboo may have very detrimental effects on the client whose ego strengths are poor. Kardener (1974) supports this particular argument against therapist-patient sex. Barnhouse's second reason is that an important part of therapy is frequently the interpretation and understanding of the client's sexual fantasies, particularly where these involve the therapist. Where these are acted out, the opportunity for interpretation is lost. Finally, the argument is frequently put forward that clients voluntarily and autonomously enter into sexual relationships with their therapists, but Barnhouse considers this invalid because of the relatively greater power of the therapist in the relationship which means that the client is frequently not in a position psychologically to refuse to engage in a sexual relationship.

Finney (1975) supports this final point and suggests that even after the

43

therapeutic relationship has officially terminated, the same objections to a subsequent sexual relationship of this nature may be made. He quotes the case of a woman who was sexually propositioned by her ex-therapist two years after terminating therapy. She felt betrayed by the therapist, expressing her feelings thus: 'A psychotherapist should not ask his patient to go to bed with him. It's taking unfair, personal advantage of knowledge that he gained in a relationship of professional trust and confidence' (p. 595). Finney also warns that seduction by a client may be an unconscious expression of hostility towards the therapist, perhaps in an attempt to equalize the perceived power imbalance. Serban (1981) supports this viewpoint and adds that should the therapist end the sexual relationship, the client's anger and hostility is exacerbated and frequently leads to lawsuits against the therapist. If these possible unconscious motivations of the client are not perceived and dealt with in therapy in a constructive way, rather than acted upon, the therapist may be said to have failed in his therapeutic task.

Sexual relationships with clients are frequently justified by therapists as being beneficial for the client and therefore in some ways perhaps an acceptable therapeutic technique. Hare-Mustin (1974) strongly challenges this assertion, maintaining that, on ethical grounds, therapist-patient sex is not an acceptable therapeutic technique despite the beneficial effects it may have for some clients. She writes: 'How can it be determined if sexual contact is indicated and the treatment of choice? And, is the therapist the most competent person to provide such treatment?' And further, 'If the therapist does feel competent to offer sexual contact to the patient . . . the obvious next question would be, does the "competent" therapist offer sexual relations to all his patients who could benefit from it, rather than just young attractive patients of the opposite sex? For example, would a male therapist be equally ready to offer himself in this technique to an old unattractive female, or male for that matter?' (p. 308). One could go further and argue that if sexual relationships with clients were seen as an acceptable therapeutic technique, the principle of informed consent should apply equally to the use of this technique as it does to any other more conventional technique. The number of clients who would agree to therapy on the understanding that this might involve a sexual relationship with the therapist must be minimal. It is probably safe to add that very few therapists, even amongst those who most enthusiastically support the value of sexual relationships with clients, would be prepared to make their intention to use this 'technique' known before therapy with a client had commenced. It must be noted that most sexual relationships with clients are formed at a point in therapy where the client has developed an involvement in and dependency on the therapeutic process and the therapist himself, and is therefore no longer in a position to refuse the relationship as easily as prior to beginning therapy.

Thus, several authors have demonstrated that there is no justification for therapist-client sex, which may be condemned on both theoretical and ethical grounds. Kardener (1974) feels that it is the therapist's unresolved needs combined with the powerful position he holds in relation to the client which may propel him into such relationships against his better judgement. Once again, the need for the therapist to become aware of such needs and safeguard against their fulfilment in the therapeutic context through consultation and supervision are emphasized.

INVOLUNTARY HOSPITALIZATION AND THE RIGHT TO TREATMENT

Although clinical psychologists are not involved in the legal processes by which people are involuntarily committed to mental hospitals, they are extensively involved in the treatment of such people as inmates in these hospitals. Because the process of involuntary hospitalization automatically involves a violation of the principle of autonomy, the therapist's responsibilities towards such patients are, if anything, more serious and extensive. The remaining principles of non-maleficence and beneficence must therefore be assiduously applied and the patient's right to autonomy within the context of the hospital must be protected as far as possible.

The issues involved in protecting the rights of individuals whose freedom has been curtailed by involuntary hospitalization have been extensively debated in the literature (e.g. Schwitzgebel, 1975; Rachlin, Pam and Milton, 1975; Miller and Burt, 1982; White and White, 1981; Cahn, 1982). The right to treatment of such patients is an issue which was highlighted in the recent Donaldson vs. O'Connor case in the United States (see Kopolow, 1976; Prettyman and Snyder, 1975) in which a mental patient successfully sued the mental institution where he had been involuntarily committed for fifteen years. He claimed that during this time he had not received adequate treatment and his claims that he was neither insane nor dangerous were rejected by the hospital authorities without an adequate assessment of their validity. The Court ruled that all mental hospital inmates have a basic right to adequate treatment during their period of hospitalization.

Difficulties inherent in the provision of adequate treatment in these cases include one which was brought up in discussion of the Donaldson case in the literature, namely the chronic shortage of staff and treatment facilities which make adequate treatment of all inmates a well-nigh impossible task at many mental institutions. The responsibility of the state to provide funding and resources necessary to correct these inadequacies was emphasized to avoid placing therapists in the impossible position of having to satisfy the state by

45

adequately treating all mental patients while being denied the state resources which would make it possible to do so.

Other difficulties highlighted by Cahn (1982) involve the fact that, frequently, effective treatment of a patient's disorder is not available. In addition, the court has ruled that the least restrictive treatment alternative be the treatment of choice, but in many cases the most effective treatment is also the most restrictive (e.g. pharmacotherapy). The therapist in the mental hospital therefore has a difficult task in providing treatment which is 'adequate' (i.e. effective) and simultaneously providing the least restrictive treatment.

A corollary to the patient's right to treatment is the simultaneous legally upheld right of patients to refuse treatment (a right which is based on the principle of autonomy). Here, one of the most pressing issues is that of the patient's competence to make such a decision regarding his treatment. Mental health professionals frequently treat mental patients without their consent with the justification that by virtue of the patient's mental state he is not able to act autonomously in making such decisions. White and White (1981) point to the potential abuses inherent in this system and assert that the judgement of incompetence should be essentially a legal one and not one to be made by treating professionals. Cahn (1982) discusses the legal ruling that treatment against a patient's will may only be administered in 'emergency' situations to prevent death or serious deterioration in the condition of the patient. He points out that the concept of emergency is however not legally defined and this presents problems for therapists in deciding what constitutes an emergency and therefore also in deciding when the emergency is over.

Several suggestions have been made as to the ways in which some of the patient's rights may be respected. Schwitzgebel (1975) proposes a contractual model for treatment decisions in which therapist and patient collaborate in drawing up a contract, specifying the goals and methods of the treatment programme, after the patient has been informed of the relative effectiveness and potential side-effects of the available treatment opinions. While this may be a part-solution to the problem, it is difficult to imagine how a psychotic patient would be able to participate in such a task and therefore there must remain instances in which the patient does not participate in this way. In these cases, it is recommended that the therapist consult with some third party, such as relations, who have an interest in the well-being of the patient, and that these people be informed of, and possibly participate in treatment decisions.

METHODS AND TECHNIQUES OF PSYCHOTHERAPY

The principles of non-maleficence and beneficence dictate that the chosen method and techniques of treatment in psychotherapy must firstly not harm the patient and secondly must benefit the patient in objectively verifiable ways. Recently there has been concern expressed about the extent to which psychotherapy does benefit clients and whether in some cases the client may end therapy in a worse position than when he started. This section examines some of the attempts that have been made to assess therapeutic effectiveness, to highlight potential dangers inherent in psychotherapy and to determine what factors guide the therapist in deciding on his therapeutic approach. Some suggestions as to ways in which therapeutic efficiency may be maximized and the outcome of therapy may be more successfully measured are also considered here.

In a review of the outcome studies to date which have attempted to determine which of the therapeutic methods and techniques are more effective, Bergin (1975) states that there is some evidence that therapy is more beneficial for clients than no treatment at all. A well controlled study showed that 65% of therapy clients showed some improvement over a certain period of time as opposed to 50% of untreated controls. However, only 5% of the control group showed deterioration over this period, while 10% of the therapy clients deteriorated. Outcome of therapy did not seem to be related to the particular methods and techniques employed by therapists, but rather to the personal style of the therapist. Generally, therapists who show high levels of empathy, warmth and genuine concern during therapy sessions produce better results, while deterioration in therapy seems to be related to therapists who are impatient and authoritarian in nature or intrusive and aggressive in their approach to clients. Thus, no specific method of therapy has been identified by these studies as being more or less beneficial than any other method in any significant way.

This failure to identify differences between approaches which relate to outcome may not be so much a reflection on the absence of these differences as of the methodological difficulties which have characterized much of the research. The primary difficulty is in devising objective criteria of successful outcome. Kisch and Kroll (1980) write about the distinction between effectiveness and meaningfulness in therapy, defining 'effectiveness' as the achievement of explicit goals as measured by objective, operationally-defined criteria, and 'meaningfulness' as the client's subjective experience of the success of therapy. Kisch and Kroll assert that, by its nature, therapy frequently cannot identify explicit goals and the outcome of therapy should therefore be measured in terms of its meaningfulness to the client. Strupp (1975) argues against this professed inability to specify therapeutic goals. He states that the failure to specify goals not only makes the assessment of therapeutic outcome impossible, which may in turn allow the continuing use of therapeutic methods which are useless or even harmful, but this failure may be unethical from the client's point of view: 'If the therapist is not clearly aware of the nature of the client's problems, the treatment objectives and the kinds of outcome by which therapeutic change can be judged, he is asking the client to engage in a journey that might lead somewhere or nowhere, a venture that is time-consuming, expensive, and demanding' (p. 40). Strupp maintains that, even in types of therapy which have broadly stated objectives such as self-realization or personality growth, it may still be possible to identify the desired therapeutic outcome against which actual outcome can be measured. Strupp developed these ideas further in conjunction with Hadley (Strupp and Hadley, 1977) into a 'tripartite model of mental health and therapeutic outcomes'. In this model it is argued that there is no consensus on the definition of what constitutes mental health, and therefore no consensus on the definition of successful therapeutic outcome. Three major participants in the dispute over these definitions may be identified as being society, the client and the therapist.

1. *Society* defines mental aberration largely on the basis of observed behaviour which differs significantly from society's norms. Therefore success in therapy is measured in terms of observable behaviour change.
2. *The client's* indicator of mental disturbance is subjective emotional distress or discomfort and his aim for therapy is the relief of this distress.
3. *The therapist* bases his judgement of mental illness on some theoretical model of ideal personality structure and his goal in therapy is to change the intrapsychic processes and/or behaviour of the client which deprive him of such a healthy personality.

The outcome of any particular therapeutic process will therefore be judged differently according to which perspective is adopted in evaluation. Strupp and Hadley therefore suggest that all three of these sets of criteria be used in outcome studies, and that therapeutic outcome should not be seen as a unitary concept but as one which may be seen from differing perspectives. The model makes no evaluative comparisons of the relative merits of the three differing aims of psychotherapy. The point is that the choice of methods of therapy for particular clients will vary according to the desired goals, which could be behaviour change, relief from distress, personality change, or a combination of any of these. If therapeutic methods are evaluated in terms of this model, therapists will be able to choose between one or another in terms of their relative effectiveness in each of these three areas. Application of this model in outcome studies, which does not yet appear to have occurred, could help to determine the validity of the claims that psychodynamic therapy, aimed at personality change, will also automatically result in relief of subjective distress and behaviour change. The model could similarly test claims that behaviour therapy aimed at behaviour change may result in relief of distress and personality change. The degree to which different types of therapy are effective in each of these areas could also be clarified, and totally ineffective, or relatively ineffective therapeutic methods could be discarded.

In the absence of such objective grounds for preferring one treatment over another, the question arises as to the basis upon which therapists currently decide on which method to adopt. Barron (1978) suggests that it is the personality variables, such as particular attitudes and values, of the therapist which determine this decision. This suggestion is confirmed by Reiss, Costell and Almond (1976), who examined the technical preferences of staff at mental hospitals and found that their preferences were an indication of the kinds of personal needs each individual wished to satisfy in his or her organizational setting. The implications of this are that therapists may tend to practise a particular method of psychotherapy more for the personal gratification which they derive out of it than for its proven effectiveness in satisfying the needs of the client, and that therapy may therefore become for the therapist an end in itself rather than a means to an end. The inherent danger is that the chosen method of therapy may be inappropriate for some clients and that therapy may be artificially prolonged by the therapist beyond the point at which it is benefiting the client. These factors may be underlying some of the negative effects leading to the deterioration in some clients reported by Bergin (1975).

NEGATIVE EFFECTS

The nature of the possible negative effects of psychotherapy are rarely examined. Robitscher (1978) suggests that the direct negative effects may include the following: 1) exacerbation of presenting symptoms; 2) appearance of new symptoms; 3) the client's abuse or misuse of therapy (e.g. developing a sustained dependency on the therapy or the therapist); 4) the client 'over-reaching' himself (e.g. undertaking life tasks prematurely; undertaking tasks beyond his resources or in other ways putting excessive strain on his psychological resources) and 5) disillusionment with therapy and/or the therapist (through the wasting of the client's resources which may have been better expended elsewhere) which may lead to the hardening of attitudes towards other sources of help or loss of confidence in the therapist which may extend to other human relationships. Robitscher notes that temporary negative effects may be necessary in the course of any successful treatment and that long-term negative effects cannot be definitively related to the treatment or treatment mistakes. More sound outcome research may well determine whether the 'temporary negative effects' are outbalanced by the potential benefit to the client in the long run, and whether certain kinds of treatment and treatment mistakes generally have negative effects.

Graziano and Fink (1973) discuss what they term 'second-order negative effects in therapy which may derive out of the process of therapy regardless of

49

which techniques or methods are employed and which they have grouped as follows:

1. *'Dropouts' from therapy* – Clients who fail to complete the process of therapy fail to derive the full benefits of the treatment and, in some cases, may experience negative effects in terms of feeling that perhaps they cannot be helped at all or disillusionment with the process of therapy. The reasons why clients may terminate therapy prematurely are encompassed within the following two sections.

2. *Labelling and the 'sick' role* – The implicit labelling of therapy clients as sick or in some way inadequate may have serious consequences for their self-concept and may lead them to adopt the 'sick' role actively, unrealistically underestimating their coping capacities. The social stigma attached to being in therapy may disrupt important relationships of the client in that friends and relations may also perceive the client as sick, inadequate and in need of 'special treatment by them. Besides this, the client's family's functioning may also be disrupted, by the stigma attached to having produced a 'mentally ill' member.

3. *Demands imposed by the professional system – Fees and schedules.* Especially for lower socio-economic class clients, the difficulties of meeting the demands for payment and attendance in therapy may result in particular kinds of negative side-effects. Fees constitute new demands on the family's financial resources and may have to be met by curtailing other expenditures, depletion of savings and going into financial and possibly concomitant psychological debt through borrowing money from the extended family or other resources. This may increase the emotional strain between family members and particularly between the rest of the family and the client for whose benefit the sacrifices are being made. Time schedule demands lead to disruption of normal scheduling which may include taking time off work and consequent loss of pay and loss of status at work.

Graziano and Fink maintain that therapists are frequently unaware of these kinds of difficulties encountered by the client, and that where these are sufficiently great the client may harbour resentful feelings towards therapy and the therapist, which, unless recognized and dealt with in therapy, may hamper therapeutic progress or lead to premature termination by the client.

In assessing the effectiveness of therapy, both the beneficial and potentially negative effects of therapy for particular clients must therefore be considered. Ellis (1980) introduces another element when he points out that in recent times, when economic resources are becoming scarce, there is increasing pressure on therapists to provide therapy that is efficient in terms of time and money as well as effective. He proposes that in order to be efficient, therapy should preferably be brief, depth-centred, extensive, thoroughgoing and preventative. The rationale for these characteristics is that besides brevity, which ensures minimum expense in terms of both time and money, therapy which is maximally efficient should also ensure that therapeutic progess is maintained once the actual process of therapy has ended. Therapies which concentrate on symptom-removal, although brief and effective, may not necessarily be the most efficient in these terms unless they also equip the client with more adequate coping mechanisms which will prevent the re-emergence of problems in future difficult situations.

It has been seen that in choosing a particular method of psychotherapy the therapist needs to balance the possibility of negative effects against the potential benefits to the client and must also ensure that the method is maximally efficient. The question arises as to whether there are any existing methods of therapy involving techniques which make them immediately unethical in these terms.

Some – such as aversive techniques in behaviour therapy – involve harm to the patient which forms an essential part of the process of treatment. It is generally accepted by behaviour therapists that such techniques should be employed only where other less harmful techniques have failed to achieve the desired results and that the degree of benefit which would result from the use of such techniques should outweigh the harm involved. In other methods, the dangers of harm are less obvious and frequently underplayed by the proponents of these methods. Examples of such techniques are those involving 'deception' of the client as in paradoxical techniques and certain strategies in family therapy where the therapist consciously deceives or lies to the client in order to achieve a desired result. Haley (1977) writes: 'If it is essential for the cure that deceit be used, it might be justified on that basis. However, one must also be concerned about the long-term effect of a person experiencing an expert as an untrustworthy person, which may be more harmful than the continuation of the symptom' (p. 203). Annitto and Kass (1979) discuss the deception involved in administering placebos in pharmacotherapy saying that therapeutic deception 'is not concious lying, manipulative deceit, or dishonest chicanery; rather it is an example of the expression of the conscious decisions made during psychotherapy' (p. 552). Thus, in some cases where benefit to the client may definitely be expected to result out of deception and where the therapist's motivation for deceiving the patient is entirely based on the desire for and expectation of this benefit, conscious and deliberate deception in therapy may be a valid and useful technique. However, as Haley asserts, it is necessary to be constantly aware of the balance between the benefit to be derived and the possible harm which could arise if the client realizes that he is being deceived.

A difficult ethical situation arises when new therapeutic techniques are being developed. Initially, in such a process, the therapist cannot be sure that the new technique which he believes may benefit clients will in fact do so or will not produce concomitant negative effects. In addition, when practising such techniques the therapist cannot claim to be competent in this practice. Obviously then there are attendant risks in the initial implementation of any new therapeutic method and, as such methods develop primarily through practice, some clients will inevitably be exposed to these risks. Advancement in the practice of psychotherapy necessitates the continuous re-evaluation of old methods and experimentation with alternative methods, but it is suggested that, in order to minimize the risk, these innovations be based on sound theoretical judgement and that the first clients who serve as the 'guinea pigs' for such innovations be regarded as research subjects. The ethical considerations applicable to research, which will be discussed in a later chapter, should then also be applicable in these situations.

This section has highlighted the dearth of definitive research on the relative efficacy of various psychotherapeutic methods and techniques and emphasized the need for such research in order to allow therapists to make treatment decisions on other than purely subjective criteria. The nature and causes of negative effects in therapy have been examined and it is emphasized that in deciding on a treatment method the possibility of such effects should be continually weighed against the potential benefit of the treatment process. The ethical validity of certain existing types of therapeutic methods has been briefly considered and, finally, the ethical problems inherent in the innovation of new techniques were examined. The major ethical problem in this area appears to revolve around the careful cost-benefit analysis (described in chapter one) of treatment methods. At present, in the light of the lack of satisfactory research into the effects of therapy, this remains a difficult task which each individual therapist must tackle within his own sphere. The major need which is identified in this area is, therefore, the need to conduct further, more adequate research into therapeutic outcome and the relative efficacy of existing techniques. In the meantime, therapists have an obligation to inform clients fully of the limits of their effectiveness.

THE CLIENT'S CONSENT

Before beginning therapy, the client must be informed of and consent to the type of treatment which the therapist is able to offer and the demands that will be made of the client in the context of this treatment. Some estimate of the cost of treatment in both time and money must be given, and frequently a 'trial period' may be agreed upon, during which the therapist may guage more accurately the possible length of treatment and the client may decide whether he finds the style of treatment congenial.

Robitscher (1978) emphasizes the importance of informing the client of potentially harmful side-effects of treatment, whether these involve emotional distress or physical discomfort. All forms of therapy, even the essentially non-intrusive 'talking therapies', involve some degree of emotional distress due to the uncovering of emotionally painful material, and this must be explained to the client who may then make an autonomous decision as to whether the benefits to be derived from therapy outweigh the distress involved in the process.

The therapist also has an obligation to inform clients of alternatives to the type of treatment he can offer, such as other therapeutic methods or even non-therapeutic support systems in the community.

These alternatives must be presented in the most objective possible way with reference to their relative effectiveness and the kinds of demands they make on the client in terms of time and money. The client may then decide on the basis of his own personal needs and limitations which of these procedures he prefers.

In order for the principle of informed consent to be applied in a way which maximizes the achievement of its main aim of protecting the autonomy of the client, several issues must be considered. These are mainly concerned with the nature of the consent which is requested by the therapist and the degree of freedom to refuse consent experienced by the client.

It is the practice in some kinds of agencies to ask clients to sign 'blanket' consent forms which place decisions regarding treatment and the release of confidential information entirely in the hands of the agency. This violates the principle of informed consent in that clients are almost invariably unaware of the implications of signing such blanket consent forms. Some authors (e.g. Ayllon and Skuban, 1973; Coyne and Widiger, 1978; Schwitzgebel, 1975) refer to the lack of clarity and confusion that may arise in situations where such blanket consent is obtained. They believe that this lack of clarity may even extend to verbal agreements between therapist and client and suggest that one resolution of this situation may be the use of written contracts, signed by both client and therapist, which clearly specify the relevant aspects of the therapy to which the client is consenting. Such contracts may be renegotiated and revised at any point in therapy at which any one or more of its elements are no longer relevant.

It has been suggested that some clients may give consent for various aspects of therapy because they are in need of help and fear that, should they refuse to give such consent, they will be refused treatment. Rosen (1977) confirmed this, through research which demonstrated that when clients applying for treatment at a psychotherapeutic agency were not told that they had the right to refuse consent, there was 100% compliance. However, when they were informed of this right, only 20% complied. In this sense, clients are coerced into signing consent forms – a situation which defeats the purpose of obtaining informed consent at all. Thus, clients should be informed that their choice is fully autonomous and that the provision of treatment will not be affected by their refusal to consent to certain aspects of the treatment.

Objections to the application of informed consent in psychotherapy arise out of therapists' fears that, if confronted by all the possible difficulties and negative effects of psychotherapy, clients may lose confidence in the treatment before being able to experience its positive aspects, and may be 'scared off' therapy or else may be so cautious of the therapeutic process that progress will be impeded. Epstein (1978) argues that, while this may be true in some cases, there is the danger inherent in some therapies of a subtle authoritarianism emerging in which the client is seen as child-like and helpless, unable to make his own decisions regarding his preferences and in need of the wiser, parent-like therapist to make these choices for him. Epstein believes that: 'It could be a boon for therapeutic efficacy to appreciate what is positive about a patient, and to recognize that an individual makes choices and takes action quite freely with responsibility for these choices and actions' (p. 87).

Indeed it is difficult to understand how the therapeutic aim of developing the client's autonomy can be helped by robbing the client of all autonomy in decisions regarding the important aspects of the therapeutic process.

CONCLUSIONS

It is apparent from discussion in this chapter that, perhaps more than in any other area of the clinical psychologist's functioning, the practice of psycho-therapy involves the careful application of all three of the basic ethical principles discussed in chapter two. The therapist experiences a degree of responsibility in relation to clients, coupled with other demands which make it difficult to realize these responsibilities. The current limitations in theory and technique also serve to complicate the ethical dilemmas confronting the therapist. The purpose of this chapter has been to clarify the nature of these dilemmas and to suggest ways of approaching them. It has been seen that the application of the rule-utilitarian approach to ethical dilemmas may prove useful to the practising therapist, and the application and usefulness of the principle of informed consent has been discussed in relation to many problem situations. It appears that there are no easy solutions to the ethical difficulties encountered by psychotherapists and that one of the major tasks of clinical psychologists as therapists is a careful and intelligent analysis of each situation and the adoption of an approach which is informed by an awareness of the dictates of all the ethical principles to which they must adhere.

4

ETHICS IN PSYCHOLOGICAL ASSESSMENT

Of all mental health professionals, the psychologist alone is expert in the administration of psychological tests. For this reason it is particularly import-ant for psychologists to maintain the highest possible professional and ethical standards in conducting psychological assessment procedures. This chapter outlines the standards of ethical behaviour required to maximize the usefulness of psychological assessment procedures (beneficence), to minimize the abuse of such procedures (non-maleficence) and to simultaneously protect the autono-my of individuals subjected to such procedures. These standards will be discussed with reference to the goals of psychological assessment, the available assessment methods and techniques, competence of the psychologist, mainten-ance of confidentiality, and the concept of informed consent as it relates to psychological assessment.

GOALS OF ASSESSMENT

Psychological assessment may be requested by a variety of interest parties for a number of different purposes. These may be broadly categorized as follows:

1. Aptitude testing – an individual may refer himself for assessment to guide him in choosing a suitable occupation.
2. Employment – individuals may be referred by potential employers in order to assess their suitability for positions in their organization.
3. Legal assessments – courts may require the assessment of individuals i) to judge criminal responsibility or ability to stand trial, ii) to assess the degree of loss of functioning in, for example, compensation claims due to head injuries resulting from accidents, iii) to assess the suitability of parents disputing custody.
4. Scholastic assessment – children may be referred for investigation of their

failure to attain normal educational standards or to assess children for special class placement.

5. Diagnostic assessment – other mental health professionals may request assessment to help determine the diagnosis of a patient.

6. Therapy assessment – this may be required to assess the suitability of a patient for a particular mode of therapy or to provide further insight into the types of intraspsychic conflicts which may need to be explored during the course of therapy.

It is apparent that the results of psychological assessment may have far-reaching implications for the future of the individual being assessed. A clear definition of the exact goals of the assessment procedure is therefore important in order to ensure that the information gained will be relevant, complete and accurate.

Besides ensuring that the goal is clearly defined and understood both by himself and by the referral agent, the psychologist may frequently be required to judge whether a particular goal is appropriate and whether his participation in assisting in this goal is ethical or not. A useful guideline in deciding on this is to consider the ethical principles of beneficence and non-maleficence. That is, the goal of assessment should be concerned with the well-being of the client and not constitute potential danger to the client. In most cases this is easy to determine. Even where an individual may be refused a job due to the results of psychological assessment it could be argued that it would not be in his best interests to occupy a position with which he would not be able to cope psychologically. The major difficulty that arises in this area is where the interests of society conflict with the interests of the individual being assessed. This is particularly apparent in legal assessments of individuals standing trial for criminal behaviour where the psychologist's assessment may result in imprisonment or commitment to a mental institution. In these cases it is argued that the psychologist's participation is justified on the basis that society must be protected from dangerous or potentially dangerous individuals and therefore assessment of such cases falls within the range of ethical behaviour.

A particularly awkward ethical dilemma may arise for psychologists who are employed by state institutions such as the judicial system (courts and prison services) and the defence force. The question for such psychologists is how to balance their responsibilities to the state, which is their employer, against their ethical responsibilities to the individuals who they are asked to assess by the state. It has been seen that any government is concerned not only with protection of the individuals under its jurisdiction, but also with the protection of its particular policies and practices based on those policies. It is possible, then, that state-employed psychologists may be asked to participate in assessment procedures which would assist the state in protecting its policies rather than in protecting the broader society. Examples of such instances range from that quoted in chapter two, of the psychologists employed by the United States defence force during the Vietnam War, to instances in which mental health professionals are called to assist the government in interrogation of political prisoners. Participation in the latter type of procedure seems difficult to defend ethically. Robinson (1974) has argued that, while psychologists have a duty to assist in protecting the broader society against 'dangerous' individuals, the definition of dangerousness should include only private harm and not political activism. The difficulty here, of course, is that political activism may include the risk of private harm as in the increasing 'urban terrorism' experienced world-wide. A strong argument against assisting the state in suppressing political dissension by conducting assessments of political prisoners is that the professional image of psychologists would be seriously damaged by psychologists who act as agents of any particular state and who are therefore seen as putting the policies and interests of that state above the interests of the individual client. Where the client does not represent any direct danger to members of the society and where the consequences of the assessment procedure would violate the principles of autonomy, non-maleficence and beneficence in relation to the individual being assessed, assistance of the state by psychologists may be viewed as directly unethical.

A further consideration in determining the goals of assessment concerns the right of the referral agent to have access to particular information about a client. It can be argued that in order to ensure the client's autonomy to a maximal extent, the psychologist must release to referral agents only such information as is directly relevant to the agent's concerns and the concerns of the client in relation to the agent. For example, an employer who requests the assessment of a job applicant needs only such information as would be pertinent to their decision on job allocation. An employer does not have the right of access to private information about the client such as his marital difficulties or intra-psychic conflicts where these would not affect his performance of any job-related tasks. Although the psychologist may acquire such information during the course of assessment it would be inappropriate for him to release this even if requested to do so by the employer.

Finally, in determining the goals of assessment the principle of non-maleficence dictates that the psychologist must also consider the indirect consequences of achieving these goals and, where possible, minimize the negative elements of these consequences. For example, when assessing schoolchildren for potential special-class placement, the psychologist must not only consider whether the child's intelligence is not sufficient for normal schooling, but also what the consequences of such placement would be in terms of the possible stigmatization, the child's loss of self-esteem and the family's reactions to the decision. As part of the assessment procedure the psychologist should consider the strengths of the child and the family and ways in which these may be mobilized in order to minimize the negative side-effects of such a decision, even where, overall, the decision could be considered as being in the best interests of the child.

It is apparent from the above discussion that the clinical psychologist's role in psychological assessment extends far beyond the unquestioning conducting of an assessment procedure at the request of any referral agent. Defining the goals of psychological assessment involves decisions as to whether the goals themselves are ethically justifiable, determining the appropriateness of requests by particular referral agents for psychological assessment, and conscious attempts to ameliorate the indirect negative effects of both the assessment procedures themselves and their consequences.

METHODS AND TECHNIQUES OF ASSESSMENT

The two major components of any psychological assessment procedure are interviewing strategies and the administration of psychological tests. Although texts on psychological assessment have traditionally emphasized the latter strategy, the importance of conducting a concise interview with the client in order to gain historical data as well as data on current functioning is emphasized by Maloney and Ward (1976): 'A well-documented history gives a context in which the client's current problematic performance can be viewed in perspective. In fact, case history data are crucial to adequate assessment of many problems' (p. 7). Anastasi (1976) also states that test scores cannot be adequately interpreted without other pertinent information about the individual.

In deciding what information needs to be gathered and which tests need to be administered it is important for the psychologist to consider both the goals of the assessment procedure and the individual who is being assessed. Method and technique need to be selected on the basis of their appropriateness both to these goals and to the individual in question.

Goal Appropriateness

A wide variety of tests exist measuring many different aspects of psychological functioning. The two crucial considerations here are those of validity (does the test measure what it purports to measure?) and reliability (does the test measure the same function consistently over time?). Before tests are made available for general use it is assumed that the designers have taken precautions to ensure that it is both valid and reliable, but it is the responsibility of the individual psychologist to ascertain by reference to the test manual that in fact this has been adequately ensured.

In addition, the psychologist must determine the exact nature of the test's purpose. Many tests measure only one particular aspect of an area of psychological functioning – for example Test A may measure immediate recall of visual material, while Test B may measure delayed recall of auditory stimuli. Although both tests A and B are measuring memory the two aspects with which they are concerned are different in many respects, and total memory functioning cannot be assessed by using only one or the other.

Thus, bearing in mind the eventual goal of the assessment procedure, the psychologist must isolate the particular areas of psychological functioning which would be pertinent to the general ability which is being assessed, and must then select tests which are appropriate to those specific areas of functioning.

Individual Appropriateness

In deciding whether it is appropriate to administer a particular test to the referred individual, the concept of standardization becomes important. Before a test is released for use, standardization studies must have been conducted to provide norms against which an individual's functioning on that test may be compared. These studies must be reported in the test manual and it is important that the psychologist ensure that the standardization sample which produced the norms constitutes an appropriate comparison group for the individual. For example, the norms of a test standardized on white, American college students may not be appropriate in assessing a Nigerian labourer who left school at the age of twelve.

The issue of test bias becomes important here. It has been widely argued in the United States that intelligence tests based on the American cultural tradition unfairly discriminate against lower-class black Americans, and that, on the basis of their lowered scores, they are denied employment and other opportunities for advancement. Anastasi (1976) agrees that certain types of cultural background have an effect on test performance and may therefore lower test results. She argues however that this is not in itself an undesirable outcome. What is important is the interpretation that is put on these lowered scores. For example, if intelligence tests are regarded as definitive measures of basic intelligence, 'culturally disadvantaged' people may be discriminated against by virtue of being seen as less intelligent. Anastasi asserts that such tests should rather be seen merely as 'behaviour samples' and it must be recognized that performance of these behaviours may be affected by a wide range of individual factors, including cultural background. She writes: 'Every psychological test measures a behaviour sample. Insofar as culture affects behaviour, its influence will and should be detected by tests. If we rule out all cultural differentials from a test, we may thereby lower its validity as a measure of the behaviour domain it was designed to assess' (p. 58). However, Anastasi recognizes two major sources of cultural bias in testing. One is where cultural factors affect performance of the tasks which the test is designed to asssess and the other concerns cultural bias which is 'built in' to the test design and content.

1. Cultural Bias in Task Performance

Performance on particular tests may be affected by factors which arise out of the individual's cultural background. These may include unfamiliarity with test-taking procedures, low test-taking motivation, poor educational background leading to reading difficulty or inadequate knowledge of arithmetic, and hostility towards authority figures of which the psychologist is representative. It is therefore important in the interpretation of test results that such facts are taken into account in order to differentiate between those whose poor test performance results from an inherent deficit in performing certain tasks and these whose performance is affected by extraneous culturally-related variables. Another way of approaching the problems is to avoid comparisons across cultural groups by developing subgroup norms, so that the individual is evaluated according to the general functioning of the cultural group to which he belongs.

Because such culturally-related sources of bias do contaminate test results, it may be argued that some tests which are particularly biased should not be used at all with clients who are at a disadvantage in relation to the test content or materials. However, the decision as to whether or not to administer such tests to certain clients may be taken more beneficially by considering carefully the aims of the assessment procedure. For example if the question asked by the referral agent is 'how intelligent is the client?' culturally-biased intelligence tests should not be used as they will not give a true reflection of the client's intelligence. However, if the question is along the lines of 'how well will the client be able to perform particular functions?' even a culturally-biased intelligence test may be useful where the relevant functions may be assessed via this test. This is because it is assumed that the cultural factors which determine performance on the intelligence test will have similar effects on performance of the functions in which the referral agent is interested.

2. Within-test Cultural Bias

Test content which discriminates against members of particular cultural groups includes the use of names or pictures of objects unfamiliar in a particular cultural milieu and stories or pictures depicting life situations exclusive to one subgroup which may lead to feelings of alienation in members of other groups (e.g. the exclusive representation of members of one racial group in illustrations). The negative effects of such alienation are particularly important because they will depress the individual's performance of particular functions which under other less culturally-biased conditions may have been far better performed. It is therefore vital, if psychological assessment procedures are to be appropriate for members of other cultural groups, that test materials and content which contain such sources of cultural bias should be reviewed and revised. Until such time as this revision occurs, psychologists must be particularly aware of the possible effects of culturally-biased content and interpret test results cautiously in the light of the possible negative effects of such content.

In summary, assessment procedures, in order to be effective, need to be carefully selected bearing in mind the particular functions of test materials, their validity and reliability, the standardization sample with which the test was developed and possible further sources of test bias particularly when assessing members of other cultural groups. Where fully appropriate tests are unavailable, the aims of the assessment procedure must be carefully considered before such tests are used and test results must be interpreted cautiously in the light of their inherent bias.

COMPETENCE OF THE PSYCHOLOGIST

It has been seen that a psychological assessment procedure includes both interviewing the client and the administration of psychological tests. For this reason, the psychologist must be competent both in interviewing strategies and in test administration and interpretation.

The purpose of the interview as part of the assessment procedure is to obtain historical data and information about current functioning which will illuminate test results and will also inform the psychologist as to the types of test which would be appropriate within the procedure. For this reason, the psychologist should, during the interview, explore all aspects of the client's past and current experience which would be of value in arriving at an accurate assessment of the client's problem. There are many ways in which failure to explore certain of these aspects may be detrimental to accurate assessment. One example of this may occur in the administration of personality tests. Many of these tests are influenced both by the client's personality or emotional state and by the client's cognitive capabilities. On the Rorschach test, for example, responses which show 'poverty of content' or which do not have an adequate form level may be indicative either of a low level of intellectual functioning or of emotional disturbance. If a client has been referred for a personality assessment and the psychologist fails to enquire about the client's educational level or intellectual facility, poverty of content in responses to the Rorschach may be incorrectly interpreted as a positive sign of depression. Such an incorrect interpretation may have serious consequences for the client who may then be treated for depression unnecessarily. Similarly, depression or other emotional disturbances may influence a client's scores on an intelligence test and if the psychologist has not enquired into the client's mental state during the initial interview, the client's intelligence will be incorrectly estimated. In addition, visual, auditory or other physical defects may affect the client's performance on any psychological test and their presence must be ascertained by the psychologist prior to testing.

It is apparent, therefore, that the competent psychologist conducts a full and comprehensive interview with the client as an integral part of the assessment procedure and is alert to any aspects of the client's functioning which may have relevance to an accurate understanding of the client's difficulties and capabilities, and to the selection of appropriate testing techniques. In addition, the interview with the client may serve as a period during which the client may familiarize himself with the psychologist and the testing procedure itself. Any anxieties about the aims and methods of the investigation may be detected by the psychologist and explored with the client so that anxiety which is situation-related may be minimized as an interfering variable in the client's test performance.

The competence of the psychologist in administering and interpreting psychological tests is obviously of vital importance. Distribution of tests and test materials is restricted to qualified test users, who include psychometricians and psychologists registered in various categories. The types of tests which may be administered and interpreted are determined by the category in which the psychologist is registered and it is assumed that psychologists registered in a particular category will, by virtue of their training, be competent in the use of particular tests. This, however, may not necessarily be the case as there is an extremely wide range of available tests and the restrictions of current training programmes make it impossible for a trainee to have exposure to each and every one of these tests. For this reason, it is the responsibility of the individual psychologist to ensure that, when administering a test which is unfamiliar to him, he familiarizes himself fully with the test's purposes, materials and methods of administration by careful study of the test manual. In addition, in both administration and interpretation of an unfamiliar test, the psychologist should, if possible, consult a colleague who has had experience with the test and who is aware of its practical uses and limitations.

Anastasi (1976) asserts that, besides familiarity with the tests themselves, clinical psychologists also need to be constantly aware of the latest developments in research into subjects such as learning, child development, individual differences and behaviour genetics, as 'test scores can be properly interpreted only in the light of all available knowlege regarding the behaviour that the tests are designed to measure' (p. 46). As in the practice of psychotherapy, clinical psychologists can therefore only be competent test administrators and interpreters if they continue their own education beyond the point of qualification by continued review of the latest developments in research.

In summary, competence in psychological assessment may be seen as incorporating all of the following factors:

1. facility in conducting interviews which elicit all information regarding the client's functioning which may have relevance to an accurate understanding of his current abilities and potential, and which will assist in the selection of appropriate testing techniques;
2. knowledge of all available tests, including newly introduced tests, and their range of intent;
3. selection of appropriate tests to be administered according to the goals of the assessment procedure;
4. meticulous administration of the test according to the instructions given in the test manual;
5. careful interpretation of test results taking into account all other relevant data, including information about the client's cultural background and life history, and recent research findings relevant to the behaviour being assessed.

It has already been made clear that the consequences for the client of recommendations made by psychologists on the basis of their assessment procedures may be far-reaching. It is the psychologist's ethical responsibility to fulfil all the criteria for competence in this area, in order to ensure that these consequences are appropriate and in the client's best interests.

CONFIDENTIALITY

The principle of confidentiality as applied to psychological assessment takes two forms. Firstly, it is essential to protect the client by protecting, as far as possible, the confidentiality of test results. Secondly, in order to ensure that tests remain maximally useful, the confidentiality of actual test content and material must also be ensured.

The first problem that arises here is to whom test results are to be communicated and the form that such communication should take. There are generally three types of interested parties who may request such information – the client himself; in the case of children, the parents or legal guardians of the child, and third parties who may or may not have been the referral agent. The need of these parties to know the results must be balanced against maintaining the security of test content and the risk of misunderstanding test scores.

It is increasingly felt that no matter the source of the referral, the client himself has a right to know the results of any psychological assessment procedures. In America it is regarded as necessary to show the client the test report so that he can comment on its contents and if necessary clarify or correct any factual information contained within it. (Anastasi, 1976, p. 53). Where the client is a child, the parents are regarded as having similar rights of access to this information.

Solomon, Kleeman and Curran (1971) consider cases where the assessment has been requested by agencies such as potential employers and emphasize the need to explain to the client prior to the assessment, the kind of information which will be communicated to these agencies. They also emphasize the importance of keeping confidential any information gathered during the interview which is not directly relevant to the purposes of the referral agent; stating that 'redundancy, unnecessary details, and extraneous matter can often be omitted without weakening the report' (p. 1568).

In all cases where the results of assessments are requested by third parties who were not the referral agent, the client's permission must be obtained before any information is released. It is apparent that the results of psychological assessment may be communicated to any number of interested parties and, especially if it is assumed that the client will also have access to the assessment report, it is obvious that the way in which test results are communicated is of central importance. The risk of misinterpretation of test scores is especially important and it appears necessary to avoid reporting raw scores. For example, in reporting on IQ testing, the client's actual IQ score should not be reported and discussion of abilities should be limited to ranges of ability rather than fixed scores. The raw scores should be stored in a separate file which would only be available to psychologists who are qualified to interpret them adequately. In addition, interpretations of test material should be presented in a clear, understandable way without the use of technical jargon, and limited to the immediate objectives of the assessment procedure.

The strict confidentiality of test protocols is an obvious necessity in the light of the above, and these should not be stored in a file which is readily available to anybody other than the psychologist who is concerned with the case. In all cases, no information on the capabilities of a client should be released without the client's knowledge of and consent to this release.

The necessity to maintain the confidentiality of test content and materials is obvious as, should these be freely available, the tests would no longer serve their purpose and would therefore be redundant. This is because many tests rely, for their efficacy, on unfamiliarity with specific test materials. Assessment of various functions would be artificially raised by the client having learned or practised the particular test task designed to measure a general ability. In some situations, for example during court proceedings, psychologists may be called upon to explain the purpose of a particular test and to justify the relevance of the test to the assessment of personal characteristics. On such occasions it is important that the general purposes and construction of the test be explained without revelation of any of the actual questions or materials which form part of the test.

INFORMED CONSENT AND PSYCHOLOGICAL ASSESSMENT

Psychological assessment procedures frequently involve, sometimes of necessity, that the client reveal personal information without being aware that he is doing so. For example, the projective tests of personality would not be effective in many cases if the client were fully aware of the methods by which his responses would be interpreted. It must also be borne in mind that any observation of the client or routine history-taking will reveal to the astute clinician information which the client is unaware of communicating. There is therefore an element of deception in assessment procedures which increases the responsibility of the psychologist to preserve as far as possible the autonomy and privacy of the client.

As in the practice of psychotherapy, obtaining the informed consent of the client for participation in assessment procedures may be useful in minimizing the degree of invasion of privacy which is frequently involved. In undergoing an assessment, the client should therefore always be aware of the general aims of the procedure and should consent to participation in procedures which have these goals. Related to this is the necessity to inform the client which parties will have access to the information gained during assessment.

Prior to the procedure the client must be informed that he may inadvertently communicate information to the examiner regarding his general functioning with the assurance that the examiner will use this information only in ways which will be relevant to the general purposes of the assessment. Also, prior to administering each test, there should be some general statement of the broad purposes of the technique. It is in this area that the psychologist needs to exercise special care to ensure that the client has enough information to make an informed decision as to whether or not to participate while simultaneously avoiding reducing the validity of the test by evoking defensiveness and resistance to the client. The amount of information which can be communicated will therefore vary according to the nature of the test.

Although some psychologists feel that obtaining informed consent from clients may increase their resistance and reduce the number of clients who agree to participate in assessment procedures this has not in fact been found to be the case. Fink and Butcher (1972) assert that 'the number of respondents who feel that a personality inventory represents an invasion of privacy or who consider some of the items offensive is significantly reduced when the test is preceded by a simple and forthright explanation of how items were selected and how scores will be interpreted . . . such an explanation did not affect the mean profile of scores on the personality inventories' (p. 638).

Thus, it appears that, far from reducing the number of clients who agree to participate, applying the principle of informed consent in psychological assessment may in fact provide the necessary reassurance for the client to feel free to co-operate fully in the assessment procedure.

CONCLUSION

This chapter has examined the ways in which the ethical principles relevant to psychology may be applied in psychological assessment. Competent and ethical behaviour in this field demands a careful and clear definition of the goals of assessment, selection of tests appropriate to both these goals and the particular characteristics and needs of the client, and accurate interpretation of results on the basis of these same characteristics. The rights of the client are to be protected by maintaining the confidentiality of test results and by obtaining the informed consent of the client before any assessment procedures are initiated.

5

ETHICS IN RESEARCH

Psychological research involves many complex ethical issues, some of which are common to research in all fields of scientific endeavour, but many of which arise out of the inevitable use of human subjects in research in psychology. The ethical dilemmas confronted by psychologists in conducting research will be examined in this chapter mainly with reference to the goals and methods of research projects. These two issues will be discussed separately although it will become apparent that they are mutually interdependent, with the goals of research dictating the methods and research methods frequently being evaluated in terms of the ultimate goals.

GOALS OF RESEARCH

The primary role and duty of any scientist is to expand human knowledge through research. The basic assumption here is that knowledge is a value in itself. In terms of the principle of autonomy, all research which expands human knowledge is ethical because it provides humans with greater understanding of and therefore control over the environment. However, some theorists assert that the question of whether some kinds of research are ethical or not should extend further than the question of whether this research would expand human knowledge. Parker (1974) writes that one should ask the question: 'Is the knowledge one wishes to acquire valuable or not, in an ethical sense? Ought one to know it?' (p. 209). His justification for asking this is that the acquisition of knowledge cannot be seen as separate from the application of this knowledge and, where knowledge may be applied in unethical ways to the detriment of society or groups within society, it may be better not to acquire the knowledge in the first place.

An example of such ethically questionable application is the development of nuclear weapons which was made possible by research into the possibility of splitting the atom. In psychology, Jensen's studies of race and IQ could be seen as ethically questionable from this viewpoint because of the potential for increased discrimination against blacks on the basis of the results of the research (see Jensen, 1973). These considerations have led Parker to assert that: 'Both the facts and the possible applications are dependent upon the aims of and goals of the inquiry; therefore, beforehand the aims and methods of the inquiry should be examined and an ethical choice made about the knowledge to be gained' (p. 209).

The argument against this assertion is that it may impede the development of science and therefore the progress of the human race. The American Psychological Association in their 'Ethical Standards for Research with Human Subjects' (1972) point out that 'it is rarely possible to predict the uses to which scientific knowledge can be put' (p. 2) and in the light of this, 'the scientist cannot appropriately be asked to limit research to topics that appear to have immediate relevance to human and social problems. Nor should every research scientist be held responsible for making research applications' (p. 2). The APA therefore supports the contention that research and the resultant gains in knowledge are values in themselves and states further that 'for a psychologist, the decision not to do research is itself an ethically questionable solution, since it is one of his obligations to use his research skills to extend knowledge for the sake of ultimate human betterment' (p. 2).

In attempting to clarify this dilemma, it may be useful to distinguish between 'pure' research and 'applied' research. In the field of psychology, 'pure' research may be seen as research which attempts to answer questions about human behaviour such as 'how do humans react when placed in a situation such as X'? 'Applied' research, on the other hand, would ask questions such as 'how can we manipulate the environment (or the person) so that person X will behave in this way'? It can be seen that in the former type of research, the researcher is concerned merely with gaining knowledge, whereas in the latter, the application of particular types of knowledge is investigated. It is apparent that fewer ethical difficulties arise with 'pure' research than with 'applied' research in that it is in the application of knowledge that the potential for harm may arise. It seems inappropriate to insist that 'pure' researchers should be concerned with the application to which the results of their experiments may be put in that, as has been stated, it is frequently almost impossible to predict what these applications may be. In fact, both good and bad applications may arise out of the same basic research findings. The Jensen study, for example, may also give rise to new approaches to the measurement of IQ, or at least a revised look at the interpretation and validity of standard IQ tests – a development which could only be seen as a positive advancement.

Thus, it is at the level of applied research that the goals of research may be more accurately judged according to their ethical justifiability. Here, the principles of beneficence and non-maleficence become important yardsticks in that the goals of research should be beneficial to human society and should not cause harm. This still remains a complex area in that, as has been pointed out in previous chapters, the definition of good and harm vary according to who evaluates the outcome. Thus, the development of nuclear weapons may be seen as unethical because the direct goal of such research is the manufacture of mechanisms which will most effectively kill large numbers of people, but such research is justified by governments in terms of these weapons' protective and deterring function. The decision to continue with such research depends on the beneficial effect (i.e. the protective function of weaponry) being seen as more important than the potential harmful effect (the destructive function of these same weapons).

It is apparent, therefore, that in evaluating the goals of research, both the intended beneficial consequences and the possible harmful consequences need to be taken into account, and weighed against one another before such research is conducted. While it is obvious that research conducted purely with a harmful aim is unethical, psychologists must be aware of the possibilities of the usage of results of research with a beneficent goal being used for harmful ends. Thus, while it is apparent that research into the best means for continuing discrimination against a group of people is unethical, it is not so obvious that research into the best ways of relieving discrimination may achieve the same harmful results, by highlighting the most powerful discriminative mechanisms within a society. Where the possible indirect negative results of research outweigh the intended positive results, it may be argued that such research should not be conducted and, where the research is conducted despite possible harmful applications, psychologists incur an obligation to minimize the potential for such harmful consequences by reporting and interpretating research results with due care and qualification.

METHODS OF RESEARCH

The primary ethical conflict in this area is that between the psychologist's duty to conduct research in order to improve the welfare of society as a whole and his simultaneous duty to protect the welfare of the individuals who participate as subjects in his research. As will be seen, the mechanism by which such conflicts are resolved frequently involves a form of costs-benefits analysis in which the costs are the potential physical or emotional distress experienced by research subjects and the benefits are the improvements or gains which may be made by society as a result of the research.

The forms of harm that subjects of psychological research may experience arise out of the necessity of placing them in situations in which they may experience failure, frustration, embarrassment, boredom and aggression, and may also force them to realize aspects of themselves about which they were previously unaware and which they find unpleasant – for example they may find themselves conforming blindly or cheating as a result of the experimental environment (e.g. Milgram's experiments (1963)). It is important for the experimenter to be aware of the possible emotional effects of his research methodology in his subjects and where possible to minimize these. Where the goals of the research necessitate inducing any of these negative experiences, the researcher must have satisfied himself that the benefits of the research outweigh these negative effects. In addition, the APA in their 'Ethical Standards for Research with Human Subjects' (1972) propose some further steps to ensure the autonomy and well-being of research subjects. These will be discussed in the remainder of this section, along with the major criticisms which have been levelled against them by other writers.

COST-BENEFIT ANALYSIS

In deciding whether the costs of a research project are worth its potential benefits, the APA recommend that the researcher reduce his own biases, which may contaminate his decision to proceed with the research, via three methods. Firstly, he should bear in mind that potential costs of research procedures may differ 'as they appear to the investigator, as they would consensually judged by his colleagues, as members of the general public might see them, and as they are seen by the research participant himself' (p. 3). They emphasize that all these differing points of view must be taken into account by the investigator when he attempts to evaluate the potential costs of his research. The researcher, in conducting such an analysis, should also obtain the advice of colleagues who will not be directly involved in the research project. This advice should be focussed directly on the ethical issues which will relate to the research participants. Finally, the APA recommend that pilot studies be conducted in which the main emphasis would be on gauging the subject's reactions to the research procedures and, where these are anxiety provoking or dehumanizing, attempts should be made to modify the procedures in order to minimize any negative effects. The APA conclude by emphasizing that no matter what precautionary measures have been taken or what advice has been received by the researcher, he remains solely responsible for the conducting of the research and for any negative effects on participants which may arise out of his procedures. Thus, the mere fact of having taken such measures does not release the researcher from ultimate ethical responsibility. It is therefore also important for researchers to ensure that all other professionals, such as research assistants, who are involved in conducting the research are aware of the ethical issues involved.

INFORMED CONSENT

The necessity to obtain informed consent from all potential research subjects for participation in the research project is emphasized in the 'Ethical

Standards of Psychologists' of the APA thus: 'The investigator should inform the participant of all features of the research that reasonably might be expected to influence willingness to participate. In addition the investigator should explain all other aspects of the research about which the participant inquires' (p. 6). In terms of this directive, the researcher needs to explain to subjects both the goals of the research and all negative consequences for the participants that may arise out of the research procedure.

It is this aspect of the Ethical Standards that has given rise to the most extensive debate in the literature on research in psychology. The major reason for this debate is that much research in psychology necessitates deception of the research subjects in one form or another. Eisner (1977) identifies two forms of deception – instances where the subject is given misleading or erroneous information, and instances where the subject is given incomplete information. In both cases the subject is not given the opportunity to give informed consent for participation in the research procedures. Eisner views this as a negative factor in that the participants thereby lose their freedom of choice. The further negative effects of the use of deception are seen as follows by Eisner: 'using deception may make the subject feel foolish or embarrassed, alter his psychological state, particularly his self-esteem, and lead to a feeling of mistrust and cynicism' (p. 234). She goes further to state that this latter feeling of mistrust has generalized in America to the point where many people are immediately suspicious of psychological research, expecting an element of deception to be involved. As it has been shown that suspicious subjects do not behave in the same way as naive subjects during experiments, Eisner maintains that the traditional use of deception in research has led to a situation where experimental results may be slanted anyway because of this developing suspicion, and that the use of deception is therefore self-defeating.

The counter-arguments to this position have been put forward by writers such as Resnick and Schwartz (1973) and Helmchen and Muller (1975) who argue that in order to avoid perceived-demand effects in research, the actual goal of any research must of necessity be hidden from research participants. An example of such situations in psychological research is the use of placebo treatment in order to measure the efficacy of new techniques of psychotherapy. It is argued that it would be impossible to measure the effects of such techniques without placebo groups which could be compared with both no-treatment control groups and the treatment group. To inform subjects that they may receive a placebo would influence their expectations and contaminate the results of the research. Even where placebo research is not involved, Resnick and Schwartz (1973) have demonstrated that fully-informed subjects behave significantly differently from deceived subjects in research and that the application of informed consent in research settings therefore makes certain kinds of research difficult, if not impossible.

Rugg (1976) has attempted to shed more light on this conflicted area by investigating the attitudes of potential research subjects towards the use of deception in research. His results showed that where no stress was involved, deception was generally regarded as acceptable, but stressful research procedures which involved deception were rejected. Thus, in a straightforward verbal conditioning experiment, deception would not be objectionable, but an experiment such as Milgram's where the subjects experienced high levels of anxiety and subjective distress would be regarded as unethical by the groups consulted by Rugg. Possible ameliorative measures in research involving deception were also investigated in this paper, and it was found that, where subjects were aware that they were involved in research but unaware of its exact purposes, careful post-research debriefing of the subjects had some ameliorative effects on the distress of the subjects.

It appears, then, that the issue of informed consent by research participants conflicts directly with the use of deception in some research procedures. The main objection to the use of deception is that it may result in negative consequences for the participants which are additional to the distress which arises out of other experimental procedures, while the major argument for the use of deception is that in some cases it may be impossible to achieve the desired results with any other design. What can be concluded from the above arguments is that, while the use of deception is not the optimum ethical choice of research design, it is occasionally necessary. According to Rugg (1976), where the research procedure does not involve stressful circumstances for the participants, the use of deception may be more justifiable, but nevertheless it must be accepted that, ethically, fully informed consent by participants is the optimum choice and therefore where possible the use of deception should be avoided or minimized. In the light of the above, the following steps are suggested as ways of evaluating research in which the use of deception seems unavoidable.

1. *Consideration of alternatives to deception* – Eisner (1977) suggests the use of simple observational techniques and 'simulation' research in which participants are placed in simulated environments for extended periods of time, as alternatives to the traditional deception design, while O'Leary and Borkovec (1978) suggest a number of alternatives to the use of placebo groups, including 'best available' comparisons, component control comparisons, neutral expectancy and counter-demand manipulation. Where a viable alternative exists to the proposed 'deception' design, this alternative would be suggested as the ethical choice.

2. *Cost-benefit analysis* – Where deception appears to be the only available option, the researcher must satisfy himself that the value of the research goal outweighs the disadvantages of the use of deception. This decision

72

should be reached after consultation with colleagues who are themselves uninvolved in the research project.

3. *Debriefing of subjects* – Rugg (1976) suggests post-research debriefing of subjects as to the actual purposes of the research and the necessity to use deception as part of the design. This would presumably help to ameliorate any feelings of resentment that the subjects may feel about being unwittingly forced to reveal aspects of their behaviour.

In summary, wherever possible, subjects should be fully informed of the factors operating in research procedures which may affect their emotional state or self-esteem and their consent to participate should be gained, but where the nature of the research requires some form of deception, researchers should ensure that the autonomy and well-being of their subjects is protected as far as possible by taking the precautions listed above.

WITHHOLDING TREATMENT AND CONTROL GROUPS

Much psychological research, especially that which involves researching new forms of treatment necessitates the use of untreated control groups against whom the efficacy of the new treatment can be compared. However, as the Working Group in current Medical/Ethical Problems (1977) points out: 'Any clinical research which is not directly for the benefit of the patients on whom it is performed poses certain ethical questions' (p. 14). Subjects who constitute control groups are not directly benefiting from the research procedures, and concern has been expressed about the ethical justifiability of withholding treatment from such groups for the purposes of research. Such withholding could be seen as violating the principle of beneficence.

This dilemma can be approached in a number of ways. Firstly, if the treatment being developed is in an area in which there has previously been no means of treatment, the control group could arguably be seen as being no worse off than before, if no treatment is administered. If the experimental treatment proved to be successful after the research, such control groups could be assured of the treatment once the research had run its course. Secondly, where some form of treatment is available it does not seem unfeasible to compare the new treatment administered to the experimental group to the previous treatment which would be administered to the control group. The only justification for introducing a new treatment is where it is superior to previous methods on one or more dimensions. In such cases it does not seem necessary to deprive the control group of treatment in order to demonstrate the superiority of a new method. Finally, in all cases where a control group is being used, the subjects who constitute this group should give consent to participate on the understanding that they would operate as controls and as such not receive the potential benefits of a newly-developed treatment method

73

until these benefits had been conclusively demonstrated through the research.

CONFIDENTIALITY

One of the most important ways of ensuring the welfare and protection of research subjects, emphasized by the APA, is the assurance of absolute confidentiality by researchers. Because of the sometimes distressing nature of what subjects reveal during research, this assurance, important in all areas of psychological functioning, is especially important here. Subjects must be informed that in reporting research results, all names and possible identifying data will be omitted. All records of research findings should be similarly censored and, for computer storage purposes, it is preferable that the subjects be assigned numbers. Where subjects are inmates of an institution, research data should not be kept in their general files, although there should be some record kept that they have been involved in a research project, because of the tendency to use the same institutional subjects in repeated research projects. Access to the original research data should be restricted to the researcher and this data should not be released to other researchers without the permission of the individual participants. All research assistants should be made aware of the importance of maintaining the confidentiality of data recorded during research.

CONCLUSION

It is apparent from discussion in this chapter that the psychologist who wishes to conduct research must be constantly alert to the ethical issues that are involved not only in the goals of his research but also in the methods by which he intends to achieve these goals. A process of careful balancing is necessary throughout the process of research. In considering the goals of research the balancing process involves weighing the anticipated beneficial uses of the research against the potential harmful uses, while in designing methodology, the protection of the welfare of the human subjects becomes important, with the balancing process involving evaluation of the potential harm to the subjects and weighing this against the beneficial outcome of the research as a whole.

6

PSYCHOLOGICAL ETHICS AND THE LAW

Professional writings dealing with the likely points of contact of the fields of clinical psychology and the law point to an at best uneasy and at worst antagonistic relationship between the two disciplines. One of the functions of professional bodies of psychologists is to prevent the intrusion into their field of expertise by external law-making bodies, by formulating rules for conduct by which their members' behaviour may be regulated. This effort on the part of such professional bodies has been relatively successful and, for the most part, self-regulation is allowed to proceed unchallenged by the broader system of justice. However, there are inevitably occasions when clinical psychologists must be accountable to the legal system for many of their practices and theories. The first of such occasions is where psychologists find themselves as the accused in public courts on charges of negligence or malpractice. The second is where they become involved, either voluntarily or involuntarily, on another level – as witnesses during civil or criminal court hearings. Both these different types of possible court involvement raise numerous ethical issues and conflicts for clinical psychologists which will be the subject matter of this chapter. It appears that the difficulty of addressing these conflicts has aroused resentment towards the legal profession in the hearts of many clinical psychologists, but it is also true that the challenges represented by legal enquiry, if taken seriously, may contribute much to the future development of the profession of clinical psychology as a whole.

THE PSYCHOLOGIST AS THE ACCUSED

Cases in which clinical psychologists are brought before the justice system as the accused normally involve allegations of harmful behaviour on the psychologist's part. This harm may be either physical or psychological and the claim is usually that the psychologist violated the principle of non-maleficence in his professional role – that is, that he did not exercise 'due care' in relation to his dealings with a client. In such cases, the court's role is to determine whether the behaviour of the psychologist was truly negligent or whether the harm was an unintentional and unforeseeable consequence of some technique or practice which the practitioner believed to be in the best interests of the client. The onus is therefore upon the clinical psychologist to prove that, as far as he could, he attempted to minimize the risks of harm to his client and that he did in fact adhere to the principle of non-maleficence.

Many of these cases concern the use of therapeutic techniques which have resulted in physical or emotional trauma for the client. Special attention has been drawn lately to those techniques which involve the 'intrusion' of the therapist onto the body of the client, such as certain types of encounter groups and 'body therapy' techniques which may involve bodily stress and pain. Recent rulings in American courts reported by Foster (1975) and Pope, Simpson and Weiner (1978) suggest that, according to the law, some such techniques are inherently negligent, regardless of the degree to which 'due care' has been exercised during their performance, so that even if it could be proved that some clients may benefit from them, the degree of intrusion by the therapist and the likelihood of resultant physical and emotional harm invariably outweigh the potential benefits, thereby rendering the techniques inherently unethical. An example of such a technique recently condemned in an American court was 'Z-therapy', developed by a practitioner named Zaslow, which involved tickling the patient until an extreme emotional reaction was provoked – presumably as some form of catharsis. The lesson to be learned from such cases is that, in developing new therapeutic methods, clinical psychologists are ethically obliged to consult widely with professional colleagues and their professional body so that a thorough examination of the potential benefits and risks of a particular technique may be conducted before it is inflicted on clients. Another safeguard would be to inform clients fully of the potential risks involved in particular treatment methods and to obtain specific, preferably written consent from the client to employ these methods during therapy. Until such time as all practitioners adhere to these ethical rules, the justice system, as ultimate arbiter of ethical and correct behaviour within society, will be obliged to intervene to provide protection for the client.

Another area of legal regulation of the functioning of clinical psychologists which has caused a great deal of concern in professional circles was highlighted in the much-publicized Tarasoff case (1974) (see Knapp and Vandecreek, 1982). This case concerned the therapist's legal duty to take active steps to prevent harm where the client is perceived as being dangerous to others. According to the APA ethical code, the clinical psychologist is obliged in such cases to inform 'appropriate professional workers or public authorities' of the client's dangerousness. However, the court's ruling in the Tarasoff case raised doubts as to whether such limited information-giving is sufficient in the eyes of the law. The circumstances of the case were, briefly, that a clinical psychologist employed by a university as a student counsellor was informed by one of his clients of the client's intention to kill a girl who had rejected his offers of a romantic relationship. Satisfied that this was a serious threat, the psychologist informed the campus police, requesting that the client be detained. He was duly apprehended and questioned by the police who consequently felt that the threat was not serious enough to justify further detention and released him shortly thereafter. Two months later the client went to the girl's home and murdered her. The girl's parents then sued the psychologist for neglect, saying that he had not taken adequate steps to ensure that the tragedy was averted. In the initial hearing, the psychologist was acquitted on the basis that he had acted in accordance with his professional ethical code, but, on appeal, this ruling was reversed and the court judged that the psychologist had in fact been negligent in that he had not warned the girl directly of the threat to her life. The arguments put forward in defense of the psychologist were that, as a therapist, he had a duty to uphold the principle of confidentiality in relation to his client and that he had, in fact, taken steps to ensure the girl's safety via the limited breach of confidentiality permitted by his professional ethical code. The judge in the case recognized the necessity for therapeutic confidentiality but stated that 'the protective privilege ends where the public peril begins'. While this statement is generally accepted by clinical psychologists as members of a broader society, the extent of the responsibility to warn potential victims indicated by the judgement is regarded with grave misgivings. The reasons for these misgivings may be summarized as follows:

1. *Questions of Competence*

Many psychologists argue that they are not competent to assess realistically the 'dangerousness' of a client, particularly where there has been no previous history of violent behaviour. Shah (1975) and Ennis and Litwack (1974) quote research which supports the conclusion that the prediction of dangerousness by mental health professionals is notoriously inaccurate and that these professionals tend to err towards overpredicting dangerousness. Shah quotes Rosen's (1954) study which showed that for every correct prediction of dangerousness there would be between 50 and 99 false positives. This tendency to overpredict may be a result of the undesirable publicity attracted by mental health professionals when a mentally-ill person who has not been detained subsequently commits a criminal act. Shah goes further to point out that even a habitual criminal who has committed numerous violent crimes in the past may not be detained on the basis of potential dangerousness alone but must actually have committed a new criminal act. He argues that it places an unfair burden of responsibility on the psychologist to decide that a client should be detained on the basis of potential dangerousness alone, especially where the clinical psychologist's assessment of such dangerousness has been shown to be unreliable.

2. Questions of Confidentiality

Mental health professionals are also concerned about the negative effects of the breach of therapeutic confidentiality involved in warning the potential victim. Taking into account the considerable difficulties in predicting dangerousness discussed above, it is likely that in many cases the client may not really carry out the intention expressed in therapy and, in such cases, the loss of trust in the therapeutic relationship may lead to the client terminating a potentially beneficial therapeutic alliance. In addition, it is felt that, were it publicly known that the therapist had a legal duty to inform the police should the client appear to constitute a threat to the safety of a third person, many clients would feel inhibited from discussing violent impulses and thoughts in therapy, while others would not enter therapy at all, thus prohibiting psychologists from offering help to such people in controlling their thoughts and impulses. The inability to help such people in therapy would in fact make them potentially more dangerous to society.

3. Risks of Harm in Warning Victims

Dubey (1974) expresses concern that several ill-effects may arise out of the duty to directly warn the potential victim, for which ill-effects the client may hold the therapist responsible. He argues that in the event of such a warning the potential victim may 'get at' the client first in self-defense, while Bersoff (1976) adds that, more commonly, the victim may abruptly terminate the relationship with the client. As a result of such possible consequences the therapist may be vulnerable to defamation of character lawsuits or be held liable for an assault on the client or disruption of one of the client's significant relationships.

Thus the legal injunction upon clinical psychologists to warn victims of a client's potential dangerousness raises a number of thorny ethical issues. Such situations are typical of those in which the clinical psychologist's ethical responsibilities to clients come into conflict with their simultaneous ethical and legal responsibilities within their broader society. There do not seem to be any easy solutions to this type of dilemma, as the psychologist remains equally bound by both responsibilities. Some suggestions have, however, been made as to how ethical decision-making in such cases may be facilitated for the psychologist.

The first issue is that of the prediction of dangerousness. Lane and Spruill

(1980) call for a set of criteria to be laid down to assist the psychologist in identifying the factors that increase the probability of dangerousness in a client who has expressed violent wishes. Shah (1975) also feels that such a set of criteria would be of assistance, but goes further to say that, as the responsibility to predict and prevent dangerous behaviour is legally imposed, the legal system should take responsibility for providing such a set of criteria. This would at least relieve the psychologist of legal responsibility for negative consequences, should the prediction be inaccurate.

In the interim, before such a set of criteria is produced, Lane and Spruill (1980) suggest that some checks on the power of therapists to make far-reaching decisions on the basis of demonstrably inaccurate predictions of dangerousness should be developed. They suggest that these checks could take the following forms: 1) obtaining several independent professional opinions regarding the possibility of danger, 2) use of existing ethical committees for consultation regarding both the prediction of dangerousness and appropriate intention, 3) alternatively, appointment by the state of one or two representative practitioners to act as consultants in this regard.

Once the therapist is satisfied that the client is dangerous, his legal responsibility dictates that he must take steps to prevent harm to the client's potential victims. However, his responsibility to the client dictates that in preventing harm to others, the therapist must inflict as little harm as possible on the client. That is, the course of action taken by the therapist should be the 'least restrictive alternative' in relation to the client. Lane and Spruill suggest that the following options be progressively attempted:

1. Attempt to talk the client out of it.
2. Change the client's environment – this includes suggesting that the client take a vacation or that he turn his weapons in to the police.
3. Enlist the help of family members or other social support systems.
4. Administer chemical restraint in the form of pharmacotherapy to be monitored through daily appointments.
5. Institute continuous monitoring or surveillance of the client with the help of family members and friends.
6. Hospitalize the client.

Any one of these options may result in a de-escalation of the immediate danger and thereby provide the time and opportunity for further therapeutic intervention. It is suggested that only in cases where all these options fail should the drastic alternatives of reporting to the police and warning of the potential victim be chosen. In other words, minimal disruption of the client's life should be the principle underlying the therapist's actions in cases of potential dangerousness.

It is apparent from discussion in this section that psychologists cannot assume that adherence to the ethical code of their professional organization makes them immune to prosecution in courts of law. Adherence to the laws of their country is inescapable and no professional immunity to such laws can be claimed. Both individual practitioners and their organizing bodies must be aware of the relevant laws affecting their practice and professional bodies are particularly responsible for providing guidelines as to appropriate ethical behaviour when society's laws and professional ethics dictate opposing courses of action. It seems clear that adherence to the law is an inescapable requirement even where such adherence may constitute harm to an individual client.However, where such a conflict exists, the individual practitioner must do all in his power to ensure that the harm to the client is of the minimum possible magnitude.

THE PSYCHOLOGIST AS WITNESS

There are two different types of situation in which a clinical psychologist may be called to the witness stand to give evidence in a court of law. The first situation is that in which a client commits a crime and the psychologist is required to give evidence during the consequent trial. The second, more common situation, is where the psychologist is required to assist the court by acting as an 'expert witness' during a trial. Each of these situations raises specific ethical questions and will be discussed separately below.

EVIDENCE REGARDING A CLIENT

The major and most obvious ethical issue raised in the first type of appearance as a witness is that of confidentiality. It will be remembered from discussion in chapter four that the privilege of confidentiality is the client's and not the psychologist's, so that if the client agrees to the psychologist's revealing aspects of the therapeutic process in court no conflict need arise. However, if the client does not grant this permission, the psychologist is bound by his professional ethical code not to reveal such information. The legal system's major concern in criminal trials is the pursuit of justice and its task is to discover the guilt or otherwise of the accused. If the court believes that evidence regarding the accused's revelations in individual therapy is essential to the realization of the court's aims, a serious conflict between the legal ethics of the court and the professional ethics of the psychologist is created.

The usual course of events in such trials is that upon being called to give evidence, the clinical psychologist refuses to do so on the grounds that it would constitute a violation of the confidential nature of the client's utterances in therapy. The judge would then announce that, by virtue of his power as an administrator of justice, he releases the psychologist from the binding nature of his duty to maintain confidentiality, and requests that the psychologist proceed to give evidence. This is the point of the real ethical dilemma. If the psychologist persists in refusing to give evidence he may himself be vulnerable to a conviction for impeding the course of justice, which conviction could imply a prison sentence. The length of this sentence will vary according to the importance assigned by the court to the psychologist's evidence in arriving at an accurate judgement. Although this is a rare occurrence, cases have been recorded in which psychiatrists and other mental health professionals who refused to testify in court on the basis of the therapeutic ethical principle of confidentiality were imprisoned for this refusal (e.g. the Caesar and Lifshutz cases discussed in Nye (1979)).

Many writers (e.g. Dubey, 1974) have argued that confidentiality in therapy is of such vital importance that psychotherapists should have the same legal immunity as lawyers and priests and should not be required by the court to expose information revealed to them in therapy by a client. However, until such time as such immunity is sanctioned by the legal system, this difficult situation will continue to require careful consideration by individual practitioners.

Possibly, a rule-utilitarian approach to this ethical conflict may clarify the issues involved and facilitate an ethical decision. Such an approach would, as has been previously illustrated, require a careful weighing of the potential harm arising to all parties affected by a decision. The ethical course of action would be that which results in the least overall harm. The parties who may be potentially harmed in the above types of situations may include the client, the client's family, the therapist, the therapist's family, other clients of the therapist and fellow members of society. If the therapist was in possession of information which, if revealed in court, would almost certainly lead to the conviction of the client, the harmful consequences of revealing such information could range from a short prison term to a death sentence for the client with consequent loss and suffering on the part of the client's family and friends. If, on the other hand the therapist refused to reveal the information, the consequences could be a prison sentence of varying lengths for the therapist. Serving a prison sentence would have harmful consequences not only for the therapist himself but also for his family and for his other clients who would be subject to an abrupt termination of the therapist's services over a certain period of time. If the client's crime were one which he would be likely to repeat were he not convicted and sentenced, there would also be potentially harmful consequences for the rest of society. All these potential sources of harm need to be carefully considered and weighed in each individual case in order to arrive at a rule-utilitarian based ethical decision. Thus, while some theorists would argue that in harming others the client forfeits his right to the protection of confidentiality, and others argue that the principle of confidentiality is absolute and never to be breached no matter the consequences, a realistic solution may be somewhere between the two and dependent on the circumstances of each individual case.

THE PSYCHOLOGIST AS EXPERT WITNESS

Clinical psychologists may be requested to assist the court by acting as expert witnesses in a number of types of court hearings. These include: 1) child custody cases, in which the clinical psychologist is asked to assess each parent's suitability as legal custodian of a minor child, 2) compensation claims in which the psychologist is required to assess the degree of psychological harm – both cognitive and emotional – incurred by one party as a result of negligence or deliberate action of another, and 3) criminal cases in which the clinical psychologist is asked to assess the mental state of the accused. While participation in trials regarding questions of criminal responsibility and fitness to stand trial has traditionally been the province of psychiatrists, there is an increasing trend in American courts towards accepting the evidence of clinical psychologists in this regard as well (Pacht, Kuehn, Basset and Nash, 1973).

It is apparent that the evidence presented in court by clinical psychologists as expert witnesses may have far-reaching consequences for the parties involved in such trials. For this reason the ethical implications of such participation and the clinical psychologist's role as an expert witness have been closely scrutinized by members of both the psychological and legal professions. The remainder of this section will examine the arguments and issues raised by both professions.

A. *The Legal Process*

The cornerstone of the legal process in the courtroom is the adversary system of presenting evidence. The principle underlying this system is that the truth may best be discovered via an argument between two people advocating diametrically opposed views or opinions. The task of a judge is to listen to the presented arguments and decide which opinion is the more accurate reflection of the facts. The role of each advocate is therefore to present evidence supporting his side of the argument. He attempts to present his own evidence as solid and incontrovertible and to simultaneously discredit the evidence presented by his opponent, showing it to be questionable or distorted. This discrediting of the opponent's evidence may be achieved either by demonstrating that the facts presented by the opponent's witnesses are false or biased, or by discrediting the opponent's witness himself, showing the witness to be unreliable, biased or misinformed.

The normal procedure by which clinical psychologists become involved in this process is that they are initially asked by one of the advocates to conduct an assessment procedure. If the results of this assessment are favourable to the advocate's side of the argument, the psychologist is asked to appear in court to present this evidence. In court he is initially examined by the advocate who called him and, via questioning by the advocate, presents what is known as his evidence-in-chief. The advocate representing the opposite side then has a chance to cross-examine the psychologist on his evidence. In attempting to support his own side of the argument the cross-examining advocate, as has been seen, is likely to attempt to discredit the psychologist and his evidence. 'This attack may be aimed at the qualifications of the witness, at his method of eliciting his facts, at his interpretation of the facts elicited and, in some cases where all else seems likely to fail, a general endeavour to produce confusion and an irritated and, hopefully, discredited witness' (Bartholomew, Badger and Milte, 1977, p. 135). Thereafter, the first advocate re-examines the expert, attempting to repair any damages to his argument rendered by the cross-examination.

The major criticism levelled at the adversary process is that it undermines objective and balanced presentation of evidence by clinical psychologists. (Anderten, Staulcup and Grisso, 1980, Poythress, 1978.) To start with, if the psychologist's assessments do not support the advocate's argument, the psychologist will not be called to give evidence and therefore will not have the opportunity to participate in the justice system at all. Secondly, if the psychologist is employed by the advocate, he is dependent on the line of questioning taken by the advocate in the courtroom in presenting his evidence. Because the advocate clearly cannot be objective in his stance, the psychologist is likely to find that his evidence is presented in a one-sided way. That is, he is not free, in presenting his evidence-in-chief, to discuss any uncertainties or ambiguities in his findings. This jars with the psychologist's ethical obligation to be objective in his professional approach. It is the task of the opposing advocate to unearth these uncertainties and ambiguities and challenge the expert witness with them. However, he is often hostile in his questioning and may not allow the psychologist time to explain why, in the light of such ambiguities, he still feels able to draw certain conclusions. The hostility of this attack is also likely to engender in the psychologist defensiveness and inappropriate rigidity in the assertion of his conclusions.

The opposing advocate also frequently calls a psychologist to support his side of the argument and the result is a 'courtroom battle' between the experts, each asserting opposite opinions and each, because of the structure of the courtroom situation, unwilling to admit to the possible validity of the other's conclusions. It is argued that the impression created by the above scenario can only be detrimental to the public image of clinical psychology as a profession. The argument is that while disagreement between psychologists as to the interpretation of data is accepted within the profession and may be healthy and productive, such debate is neither productive nor desirable in the courtroom where neither professional feels able to allow any validity to the points made by the other without feeling that his own credibility has been in some way undermined.

Poythress (1978) argues that an alternative to this undesirable system would be for the clinical psychologist to be appointed by both sides in litigation so that he could deliver a truly objective opinion in court. The argument against this is put forward by Bazelon (1974 and 1975) who argues that it is precisely because two psychologists may differ in their assessments of the same case that the adversary system is vital to maintain. He argues that an assessment by one clinical psychologist may be subject to personal bias or other subjective influences and that the adversary system which pits one professional against another is the best method of deciding which assessment is more valid. It does seem, however, that two psychologists who hold initially opposing opinions may come to an agreement if they consult professionally with one another. This agreement will never be reached in the courtroom where the issue at stake is which psychologist will 'win'. Perhaps, the ideal solution is for a panel of two or more psychologists to be appointed jointly by both parties in a case, to consult together and reach agreement on the assessment of the case before court proceedings begin. This is in fact the procedure in South Africa in criminal cases but has not been extended to civil cases.

B. *Competence of the Psychologist as an Expert Witness*

It has been seen that the major focus of the cross-examining advocate during a trial is to challenge the competence of the expert witnesses called by his opponent. Both the credibility and competence of the expert as an individual professional, and the effectiveness of his techniques are brought into question. Much debate as to the questions which psychologists (and other mental health professionals) are competent to answer may be found in the literature.

In order for witnesses to be granted 'expert' status in legal proceedings, it must be accepted that by virtue of their specialized training in a particular profession they have access to knowledge which is beyond the knowledge of the average layman (Pacht et al, 1973). Because of this knowledge, it is assumed that they will be able to enlighten the judge on matters of fact which will be of assistance to him in assessing the merits of a particular case. Ennis and Litwack (1974) add that in order for the expert's knowledge to be useful to the court, the 'facts' presented as evidence by the expert must be both reliable (that is, generally agreed-upon within the profession) and valid (that is, accurately reflect reality). Criticisms of mental health professionals' competence to assist in legal proceedings have been made on the basis of what are seen as deficits in all the above requirements for expert status. That is, it is argued by some writers that the knowledge available to mental health professionals by virtue of their training does not equip them to answer certain questions any more competently than can the average layman and that the methods of assessment used by such professionals do not allow them to arrive at 'facts' which are sufficiently reliable and valid to assist the court.

The major focus of criticism has been on the contribution of mental health professionals to trials in which the criminal responsibility and fitness to stand trial of the accused are in question. A brief discussion of the legal rulings with regard to criminal responsibility is necessary as background to discussion of this issue.

In the eyes of the law, an insanity plea is accepted as a defence against criminal responsibility. It is in such cases that mental health professionals become involved in the attribution of criminal responsibility. For many years the McNaughton Rule (1843) on the insanity defence was accepted in guiding judgements in such cases. This rule reads as follows:

> '. . . it must be clearly proved that at the time of committing the act, the party accused was labouring under such a defect of reason from disease of the mind, as to not know the nature and quality of the act he was doing; or if he did know it that he did not know that what he was doing was wrong' (Weihofen in Leifer, 1964).

The major problems experienced in the application of this rule was its reliance on the concepts of 'right' and 'wrong'. Mental health professionals complained that these concepts are moral rather than scientific in nature and that they were therefore not competent to offer any meaningful contribution in assessing the individual's knowledge or conceptualization of right and wrong. A number of revisions of the McNaughton Rule appeared, the most well-known and widely applied American ruling being embodied in the Durham decision of 1954. The essence of this decision was that criminal responsibility could not be ascribed if the criminal act was the product of a mental disease or defect. In South Africa, the Criminal Procedures Act of 1977 states that criminal responsibility cannot be ascribed where, by virtue of a mental illness or defect, the accused was *either* not capable of appreciating the wrongfulness of his act *or* was incapable of acting in accordance with such an appreciation. While these rulings removed the obvious moral overtones contained in the McNaughton Rule and seemed to be more conducive to 'scientific' evaluation of criminal responsibility, several writers argue that the attribution of criminal responsibility does and must remain an essentially moral and social question. They argue that the ascription of criminal responsibility has now been effectively and inappropriately put in the hands of mental health professionals.

85

The reason for this is that in cases where insanity has been put forward as a defence, the mental health professional is asked to make a diagnosis of the accused, that is to decide whether the accused is normal or suffers from a mental illness. The diagnosis of the accused is then presented to the court as part of the evidence of the mental health professional as expert witness. The arguments against allowing the mental health professional to present such a diagnosis as evidence are twofold.

Firstly, Ennis and Litwack (1974) argue that a psychiatric diagnosis is not an objective externally-verifiable medical fact such as high blood pressure, but is a much more subjective judgement which is prone to the professional's personal biases and preferences. They present research which shows that mental health professionals disagree as to the necessary and sufficient type and number of symptoms for various diagnoses and therefore argue that a diagnosis is unreliable. In addition, they argue that a diagnosis of schizophrenia, for example, may be made of two people who manifest entirely different behaviours; therefore diagnoses are not valid – that is, they do not relate directly to objective consistent external realities. As a result of the demonstrable unreliability and non-validity of psychiatric diagnoses these authors assert that such diagnoses should not be admissable as evidence in court.

Secondly, the presentation of a diagnosis in court does not inform the layman in court hearing the evidence as to what behaviours may be expected of a person suffering from that form of mental illness. The result of this, according to Leifer (1964) and Morse (1978) is that the court must depend on the mental health professional to make the link between the client's mental illness and his criminal behaviour. In other words, the court is forced to ask the mental health professional to ascribe criminal responsibility. The above writers maintain that the training and knowledge of the mental health professional does not equip him to make such a decision any better than can the layman. The reason for this is that there is no proven consistent relationship between mental illness and criminal behaviour. Not all mentally ill people are prone to commit criminal acts and not all criminal acts, however bizarre in nature, are committed by mentally ill people. In addition, mentally ill people may commit criminal acts which are not directly related to their mental illness. Thus, the mental health professional's training in the identification and treatment of mental illness does not imply expert knowledge of any relationship between mental illness and criminal behaviour. Rather, the particular circumstances of each case need individual consideration, and the decision as to whether or not the criminal act was caused by the mental illness depends on the nature and circumstances of the crime as well as on the nature of the particular symptoms manifested by the accused. It is argued that this connection between symptoms and crime may be established as accurately by the well-informed layman as by the mental health professional.

The argument is, therefore, that mental health professionals are not 'expert' at the ascription of criminal responsibility and that they should therefore not be asked to answer questions relating to such responsibility. Even the ability of the mental health professional to assist the courts by diagnosing the accused is questioned in the light of the questionable reliability and validity of such diagnoses. What then is the role of the mental health professional in such cases? Is the mental health professional's knowledge and competence of any value at all to the court? The answer to the latter question is a definite yes. It is agreed by most legal writers that mental health professionals are competent and qualified to elicit and identify various symptoms of mental illness such as hallucinations, delusions, etc., which *may* have bearing on the criminal behaviour of the accused. The role of the mental health professional is therefore not to diagnose the accused for the court, but to interview the accused, elicit symptoms and then to describe the nature and extent of the patient's symptomatology. Any connection between the crime and the accused's symptomatology is then the court's duty to decide. The point being made is that questions relating to the client's mental state are questions which fall within mental health professionals' range of expertise and must therefore be addressed by such professionals, whereas questions relating to the ascription of criminal responsibility are legal questions and are not specifically within the range of the mental health professional's expertise.

In the same way as the diagnostic procedure is subject to criticism on the basis of its reliability and validity, so too are psychological assessment techniques, including the construction and administration of psychological tests, submitted to close critical scrutiny by advocates who hope to prove that these techniques are not sufficiently objective and 'scientific' to allow valid conclusions to be made on the basis of data derived from them. It has been seen that the legal process has little tolerance for ambiguity or subjectivity in relation to the giving of evidence, and, for this reason, projective tests of personality which require an individualized and potentially subjective mode of interpretation are not highly regarded, coming under heavy attack in cross-examination. Anderten, Staulcup and Grisso (1980) point out that this low regard for projective techniques may constitute an ethical conflict for clinical psychologists requested to conduct psychological assessments for legal purposes. This is because, according to professional ethics, no method which is potentially useful in arriving at a thorough understanding of the client must be ignored when conducting an assessment procedure. Many psychologists regard projective tests as being potentially useful sources of data and few would tolerate the ignoring of positive signs of pathology revealed by these tests. Not to present such evidence in court would seem to them to be negligent and professionally unethical. However, the denigration of such tests by an opposing advocate on the basis of their subjectivity and questionable reliability may undermine the credibility of the psychologist's evidence in toto, thus potentially rendering more harm than if the tests had never been used or presented as evidence. For this reason, many writers (e.g. Bartholomew, Badger and Milte, 1977) advise against their use as court evidence, recommending that only those testing techniques with the most solid research foundation be selected in conducting medico-legal assessments.

The conclusions and recommendations made by psychologists on the basis of their raw data are also subject to questioning in court. In several legal papers and books (e.g. Ziskin, 1975; Poythress, 1978) specific advice is given to advocates not to accept at face value the conclusions presented to the court by psychological expert witnesses. Advocates are advised to question closely the validity of the psychologist's findings and conclusions and to familiarize themselves with published research findings which cast doubt on the reliability and validity of all the clinical psychologist's methods of investigation. These research papers are to be presented in court as a means of undermining the psychologist's conclusions based on these methods of investigation. The objection to this method of cross-examination is that it is impossible for the psychologist to be familiar with all published research and he therefore may not be able to provide a balanced opinion on the findings with which the advocate challenges him. There are methodological problems inherent in many of the research studies which may be so used and without the opportunity to examine the research himself, the psychologist will not be able to comment professionally on the validity of these research findings. It is however not only wise but an ethical requirement that the psychologist giving evidence in court be familiar with and able to refer to major research studies concerning the' techniques he has used and the conclusions he has reached on the basis of these techniques. This ensures that his conclusions will be more accurate, and that he will be able to answer such challenges from the advocate in a professional manner. Loftus and Monahan (1980) have clearly illustrated the ways in which the results of well-conducted psychological research may be of assistance in legal inquiry.

The final level of attack on competence represented by the cross-examining advocate is, of course, the critical examination of the expert witness's training, qualifications and experience, and attempts will be made to demonstrate that these are not sufficient for the witness to make expert conclusions about the issues under examination in the courtroom. For example, the clinical psychologist presenting evidence of a neuro-psychological nature must demonstrate that he has had training and experience in the assessment of brain damage sufficient to allow him to express an expert opinion on the presence or absence of organic impairment in the client.

The foregoing discussion in this section has detailed the ways in which the clinical psychologist's competence may be questioned in court. Clinical psychologists are largely well aware of the limitations of their methods of investigation and ability to derive accurate conclusions in many areas, and research is constantly being conducted to evaluate and refine the effectiveness of various techniques and decision-making procedures. Individual practitioners understand that until such techniques have been perfected they must make do' with using the best available methods, while constantly endeavouring to improve their own competence by keeping informed of latest developments within their field of expertise. However, despite this broad awareness, criticisms of mental health professionals by legal professionals often focus on the fact that, in court, mental health professionals are reluctant to admit to their limitations, pretending to a degree of expertise which they have not yet acquired (Bazelon, 1975). Perhaps it is the insecurity of working in a field where the state of knowledge is in a developing, as yet imperfect state which leads to this defensive, rigid attitude or perhaps it is the perceived hostile nature of the adversary system. Whatever the reason, it is undoubtedly true that to pretend that current methods of psychological investigation are infallible and that conclusions based upon them are absolute fact is not only unwise within the legal system but professionally unethical. In order to adhere to the professional ethical principle of competence, clinical psychologists should ensure before they embark on an assessment for legal purposes, that they are competent to conduct such an assessment – i.e. that they have the relevant training and experience. Their conclusions should be well-founded according to the latest research findings' in the field and they should not hesitate to admit to the limitations of their expertise and the imperfect state of knowledge in their profession as a whole. Anything short of this constitutes unethical behaviour.

ETHICAL BEHAVIOUR DURING LEGAL PROCEEDINGS

It is apparent from much of the previous discussion that the clinical psychologist who appears as an expert witness in court can expect to face a concerted attack by the cross-examining advocate whose aim will be to discredit the competence of the psychologist and the efficacy of his professional methods. In discrediting the individual practitioner, the advocate is also, in a sense, attacking the profession of clinical psychology as a whole. Thus, the psychologist in the witness box represents not only himself but also his profession. Behaviour of the clinical psychologist during legal proceedings should therefore be scrupulously ethical and professional. Guidelines for psychologists during the pre-trial, courtroom and post-trial phases of the legal enquiry have been put forward by several authors (Brodsky and Robey, 1972; Bartholomew, Badger and Milte, 1977; Nichols, 1980; Anderten, Staulcup and Grisso, 1980).

a) Pre-Trial Behaviour

In the same way as clinical psychologists have an ethical obligation to ensure that they are competent in the administration of psychological assessment and treatment techniques, they are equally obliged to prepare themselves for court appearances so that they behave competently and professionally in these settings. It is recommended that specific training in medico-legal procedures and the nature of the legal process as a whole be included in basic training programmes for clinical psychologists. Where an individual practitioner has not had such training, he must consult with the advocate by whom he was appointed to ensure that he is aware of these basic facts.

During the assessment procedure, consultation with professional colleagues is recommended as a means of limiting bias and subjectivity in interpreting data and drawing conclusions regarding the case. Meticulous record-keeping is essential so that precise dates, times and contents of meetings with the client may be easily recalled during the trial. These records must never be destroyed or altered in any way and must be an honest and complete account of the interactions between the psychologist and the client.

The client must be made fully aware of the purposes of the assessment procedure and the use to which any information given to the psychologist is likely to be put. He must be explicitly informed that his interviews with the psychologist are *not* confidential and will be revealed in court or, at least, discussed with the advocate. After the assessment is completed, the psychologist should personally inform the client of his findings and outline the manner in which these findings will be presented in court.

The psychologist may write a report on his assessments, to be admitted as evidence during the trial. Such a report should be complete but concise, detailing the aims of the assessment, the frequency and nature of meetings between the psychologist and the client, the methods and results of investigations, and the conclusions derived on the basis of these investigations. Conclusions must be phrased in non-technical, understandable language and must address all the major issues requiring investigation in the particular case. Where data has been equivocal or where there are remaining areas of uncertainty the report must make these clear.

Once the report has been submitted to the advocate, the psychologist must consult with the advocate as to the way in which his evidence will be led in court. The psychologist is obliged to ensure that the advocate understands fully the psychologist's methods and conclusions as there is often neither the time nor the opportunity during the structured courtroom situation to correct misrepresentations of psychological data by a misinformed advocate.

b) Courtroom Behaviour

1. The Nature of Psychological Evidence

The first issue of which clinical psychologists as expert witnesses must be aware is the distinction between essentially legal questions which they are not competent to answer and questions which relate to their field of expertise which they are competent to answer. An example of an essentially legal question is the question of criminal responsibility discussed earlier. The clinical psychologist should not attempt to answer such questions, pointing out to the court that they are beyond his limits of expertise. If there is any doubt as to which questions are legal rather than psychological, the psychologist must consult with his advocate in order to obtain clarity on this issue.

Essentially, the clinical psychologist is qualified to draw conclusions about the mental state of an individual. These conclusions are based on investigations which include observation, interviewing, and the administration of psychological tests. Interpretations of data derived via these methods are made on the basis of theoretical knowledge. The psychologist should therefore be prepared to answer questions relating to the nature of his investigations, the data derived from them, and the theoretical knowledge which led to his coming to certain conclusions about the individual on the basis of this data. Where necessary, he should support any aspects of his investigations and conclusions with reference to relevant research findings.

2. Presentation of Psychological Evidence

The psychologist's method of presenting and discussing his evidence in court must be objective, clear and to the point. Technical jargon must be avoided and concepts explained in understandable layman's terms. The principles underlying the aims and construction of psychological tests must be explained in enough detail to make their usefulness and efficacy apparent, without the revelation of actual test content which might jeopardize the confidential nature of test material.

In answering questions put to him by either of the advocates in the case, the psychologist must be honest and direct. He must answer only the question which was asked and not elaborate beyond the point necessary for clarity. Answers to questions must be addressed to the judge and not to the questioning advocate. Before answering a question it is essential that the question be clearly understood and the psychologist may ask that a question be repeated or rephrased if such clarity is lacking. The psychologist must never appear to be too strongly advocating a particular position and must readily admit to the limitations of his expertise. Where the answer to a question is unknown, the psychologist must say so and not attempt to deflect the question or give an approximate guess as an answer.

The demeanour of the psychologist throughout his appearance as a witness must be polite, neutral and undefensive. He should maintain a calm, open attitude even in the face of aggressive and hostile questioning by the cross-examining advocate. On no account should he react angrily to such cross-examination.

c) Post-Trial Behaviour

The competent and professional clinical psychologist accepts the court's decision in a case unemotionally even if the cross-examining advocate has succeeded in distorting his evidence so that his opinion and recommendations are not upheld. A post-mortem of the court proceedings in consultation with the advocate may be useful as a learning experience.

CONCLUSION

Encounters with the law, whether as the accused or as an expert witness, have been seen to be potentially traumatic experiences for individual clinical psychologists. In both cases, it is the psychologist's competence in his professional role which is most strongly brought into question. Many psychologists experience a negative reaction to the challenges of legal enquiry and become defensive and resistant to all processes of the law. A more productive response may be for both individual practitioners and the profession as a whole to give serious attention to the kinds of questions the law is asking of clinical psychologists as many of these questions are of the kind that the profession may do well to ask of itself. Where encounters with the legal process reveal discrepancies between the aims and functions to which clinical psychology aspires and its current methods of fulfilling these aims and functions, an unthreatened, objective appraisal of these discrepancies may lead to the kind of positive self-appraisal which can only benefit the future development of the profession as a whole.

7

PROFESSIONAL CONDUCT AND PROFESSIONAL RELATIONSHIPS

In the discussion of the role of professional bodies for psychologists in the Introduction, it was pointed out that one of the functions of such bodies is to promote public trust and confidence in the profession by regulating the conduct of individual practitioners. The ethical justification for this function of professional bodies is that without such confidence in the profession, members of the public who are in need of its services would be less likely to seek and acquire professional aid.

It therefore seems necessary that, in discussing ethical behaviour of psychologists, some attention must be given to the necessity of establishing and maintaining a particular public image of psychologists which will inspire confidence in members of the public who may require psychological treatment. While many of the directives discussed in previous chapters, particularly those to do with confidentiality and informed consent, may contribute significantly towards establishing and maintaining such an image, there are other areas of the psychologist's functioning not directly related to treatment of clients, such as the administration of the psychologist's practice and the way in which psychological services are made known to the public, which must also be regulated in order to protect this public image. It is with these issues that this chapter will be concerned.

The two primary aspects of a desirable public image which need to be communicated seem to be firstly the profession's primary concern with the psychological well-being of the community within which it operates and, secondly, its competence to promote this well-being.

With regard to the first issue, the profession as a whole and individual psychologists must be seen as holding the client's welfare as a primary consideration and not be seen to promote their own self-interest at the expense of the interests of their clients. For this reason, the profession must avoid being viewed as in any way exploitative, either materially or emotionally, of the public who may at some time constitute its clientele, and must be seen as willing to co-operate with other related professions where this would be in the best interests of individual clients. The second issue relating to competence of the profession as a whole to achieve its aims and adequately fulfil its service functions implies that the profession must make public the standards of competence it requires of its members and must be seen to take appropriate steps to ensure that these standards are maintained. It is essential that the public believe that any individual member of the profession whom they consult will be competent to assist them, and it is the profession's responsibility to ensure that this belief is not only widely held, but justified.

Thus, a professional body for psychologists must regulate against exploitation of the public by individual professionals and must ensure that the behaviour of practitioners does not in any way bring the competence of the profession as a whole into question. Recommendations which a professional body may make in this regard will be considered under the two major headings of Exploitation and Competence in the remainder of this chapter.

EXPLOITATION

In this section, in which regulations aimed at preventing the exploitation of the public will be discussed, three major areas in which potential exploitation may occur, will be considered. These are: remuneration for services, public statements, and co-operation with other professions.

Remuneration for Services

While it is obvious that psychologists like any other professionals, depend on remuneration for their services for their livelihood, it is important that they are not and do not appear to be primarily concerned with personal material gain. Therefore, there need to be regulations which govern both the legitimate services for which remuneration may be received and the extent of this remuneration.

As a general rule, psychologists should be remunerated, in their professional capacity, solely for those acts which are directly beneficial to an individual client or clients. A broad range of services may be offered, including psychotherapy, psychological assessment, supervision of professional colleagues, assessment and expert advice in legal proceedings, and professional consultation. The extent of the remuneration which may be received for each of these services should be determined by the regulating professional body and individual practitioners should not exceed these limits. Clients should be informed in advance of the fees for services to be offered and the APA in its 'Ethical Principles' recommends that 'Psychologists willingly contribute a

94

portion of their services to work for which they receive little or no financial return' (Principle 6(d)).

The receipt of commission for the recommendation of particular services or wares and the payment of commission by psychologists to agencies or individuals for the referral of clients to their services is generally regarded as unethical. In addition, the South African ethical code does not permit tendering for an appointment by a psychologist.

These regulations are all aimed towards reducing financial competition between psychologists, in order to maintain the image of the profession of psychology as being non-exploitative and concerned primarily with the welfare of the client.

Public Statements by Psychologists

The manner by which psychologists make themselves known to the public is obviously extremely important in creating and maintaining a particular public image.

One of the major concerns here is the prohibition of advertising which consists of any statement about the quality of services to be offered by a psychologist or of any endorsement of such services by clients or agencies. The justification for such a prohibition is firstly that such advertising is by its nature potentially exploitative, particularly as it would be aimed at an audience whose psychological resistance is low and therefore very susceptible to suggestions about quick and effective cures for their distress. Secondly, such advertising by individual practitioners is obviously aimed at personal gain for the practitioner by acquiring more clients and therefore undermines the image of the psychologist as being concerned more with the client's interests than with his own.

The ways in which psychologists may make their practices known to clients differ from country to country. In America, psychologists may publicly announce their services where such an announcement is limited to the psychologist's name, qualification, address and telephone number and types of services offered – e.g. psychotherapy, group therapy, marital counselling, etc. However, in South Africa, all such public announcements are prohibited and, when beginning practice, the psychologist is limited to informing only other professionals who are registered with the Medical and Dental Council and institutions and agencies which offer psychological services. A psychologist's name may not be listed along with his qualification in any public arena including newspapers and magazines, so that he as an individual is not made directly known to the public. In addition, nameplates outside the offices where a psychologist practises are restricted in terms of size and location so that they do not attract the attention of the general public and thereby constitute advertising.

While these latter regulations are understandable and justified in that they prevent competition amongst psychologists to be interviewed in the media and develop extravagant signs and notices advertising their services, which would again undermine the desirable image the profession wishes to maintain, it does not seem that merely announcing services to the public through the means of, for example, a newspaper, would necessarily constitute advertising. As in the American system, such announcements could be viewed as merely one way of providing information to the public as to the kinds of services which are available, and where they are located. As an alternative to the use of newspapers, a booklet could be produced by the professional body which would provide a list of psychologists available, the services they offer, and the areas in which they are located and this could be distributed to be displayed in places such as doctor's waiting rooms and the waiting rooms in hospitals and other health institutions. While not excluding the possibility of recommendation of particular psychologists by other professionals, such a measure could increase the potential client's choice of psychologist by providing him with more complete information as to the services which are available than could an individual practitioner consulted by the client. A further advantage of such a booklet being produced by the professional body would be the possibility of directly regulating the size and nature of each individual practitioner's announcement.

Co-operation with other Professionals

In order to provide the best possible service to the client the psychologist needs to be fully aware of the functions and competence of members of other related professions, and, where the services offered by such other professionals may contribute to the client's welfare, the client should be referred to these practitioners. Examples of professionals whose services may complement those of the psychologist include medical general practitioners, psychiatrists, social workers, occupational therapists and speech therapists. In order to maintain good working relationships with these other professionals, psychologists need to be aware of their traditions and practices and to respect these. It is unethical for a psychologist to publicly undermine the services or quality of services offered by other professionals whether this is done directly to enhance the status of his own profession or not. Where a client consults a psychologist while already receiving services from another professional, the psychologist must not offer his services until he has informed the other professional concerned of the referral and has come to an agreement regarding the case, and the responsibilities of each professional with regard to the case. In summary the principle of beneficence dictates that cordial and respectful relationships with other professionals must be maintained by psychologists and not undermined in public, in order to provide the client with the best possible services.

COMPETENCE

It has already been indicated that one of the hallmarks of a profession is that it ensures the competence of its members by setting standards for basic qualifications and entrance into the profession and standards for ethical conduct by its practitioners. The maintenance of trust in the competence of its members is therefore one of the most important functions of a professional body. In order to maintain this trust, individual psychologists must be prohibited from undermining this and, for this reason, most professional bodies of psychologists prohibit 'casting reflection explicitly or implicitly upon the probity or professional reputation' of any other psychologist (Government Gazette, 1979, R.437). Where a psychologist becomes aware of unethical or unprofessional conduct on the part of a colleague, the APA recommends that he first attempt to rectify the situation himself, and, where this does not succeed, then report the psychologist concerned to the professional regulating body.

In addition, in order to ensure the optimal functioning of the profession as a whole, it is desirable that psychologists report any new procedure which they have developed and which appears to be effective, in the psychological literature so that the general standard of professional services may be advanced. No psychologist may therefore claim to have a 'secret remedy' which he maintains for his exclusive use.

Finally, especially in reporting on research, the significant contribution of any colleague to one's own work must be acknowledged in the appropriate manner and all professional competition must be limited to the psychological literature. Public competition or professional jealousy undermines the general image of the profession because it frequently involves casting aspersions on the competence of other practitioners within the profession.

SUMMARY

This chapter has considered the public image of the profession of psychology and the functions of a professional body in promoting this image. It was proposed that the two major elements of a desirable public image for clinical psychology are the non-exploitative nature of the profession and its competence to fulfil the functions for which it was created.

The kinds of regulations developed by professional bodies for psychologists which are aimed at communicating and maintaining this public image were discussed in terms of their content and ethical justification.

8

THE SOUTH AFRICAN CONTEXT

It appears that, while the ethical principles to which psychologists should adhere are universally applicable, as are the functions which they are required to perform, the social milieu in which they are located will give rise to particular difficulties in fulfilling these functions in accordance with ethical principles. Thus it can be expected that, by virtue of the unique social structuring of South Africa, South African psychologists will be confronted with difficulties which are different from those in other countries and the details of an ethical code derived for psychologists in a different country such as America will not necessarily be adequate in guiding South African psychologists in ethical decision-making.

This chapter examines two of the major aspects of South Africa which distinguish it from other Western countries, and outlines some of the particular problems which are posed for psychologists by these aspects. The first to be considered is the socio-political structure of the country which is based on the principle of racial segregation, while the second concerns the composition of the population which consists of a minority of white people of European origin and a majority of black people, the bulk of whom originate from an indigenous, African cultural background considerably different from the Western cultural background. Initially these two aspects will be considered separately, but it is apparent that the effects that they have on the psychologist in his functioning must be interactive and for this reason, in the final section of the chapter, they are considered together.

THE SOCIO-POLITICAL CONTEXT

It has been noted at various points that there exists an inevitable tension between the ethical principles of autonomy, non-maleficence and beneficence, to which psychologists are committed in their practice, and societal norms, values and customs which may not be consonant with these principles.

98

Psychologists are constantly faced with the difficulty of developing the capacity for free choice and autonomous action in clients within societies in which practices such as discrimination on the basis of sex, race, religion and political ideals, mitigate against such individual autonomy. Whilst these difficulties are inherent in all societies to a certain extent, they are particularly pronounced in countries where discriminative practices are not merely customary, but lodged in the political and legal structures of the society and therefore less amenable to questioning and possible reform. In this section, the nature of the conflict between the psychologist's ethical principles and the South African socio-political system will be outlined and the types of difficulties confronted by South African psychologists as a result of this conflict will be discussed. It appears that the particular socio-political setting in South Africa has a bearing on the psychologist in his professional functioning on two levels. Firstly, it has implications for the mental well-being of the inhabitants of the country (who may constitute the psychologist's clientele), and, secondly, it influences the psychologist's functioning in his relationships with the society as a whole, with the institutions within which he may work and with individual clients. These implications will be further discussed in this chapter but it appears necessary first to outline briefly some salient features of the South African socio-political situation.

THE SOCIO-POLITICAL STRUCTURE OF SOUTH AFRICA

While a comprehensive analysis of the nature and origins of the complex socio-political structure of this country is impossible within the scope of this book, it may be possible to identify some of the major elements operative within the society which have relevance to the particular difficulties experienced by South African psychologists. Many of these difficulties appear to arise out of the policy of racial segregation which has been operative in the country for over thirty years, and which influences almost all aspects of social interaction and development.

The development of this policy finds its roots in the colonial history of the country. The white colonists gained political dominance by conquest and were responsible for developing and controlling the economy, using black race groups as the labour base upon which the economy was founded. With the discovery of mineral wealth in the late nineteenth century, South Africa became a rapidly developing and industrializing country, but the colonial pattern of exclusive white control of the political and economic spheres was maintained. This pattern became legally enforced state policy in 1948 which ensured that white dominance in political and economic decision-making has persisted until the present day. The distribution of labour and benefits within the country has therefore remained unequal and divided along racial lines. The cheap labour force on which the economy is dependent has been ensured by the development of the legally monitored black migrant labour system. Concomitantly, economic benefits are maintained largely within the white group with other groups receiving reduced services on all levels including housing, health services, education and welfare facilities. The entire system has been protected by enforcement through the legal apparatus and by the denial of effective political rights to other race groups, thus reducing potential threat to white domination and control in the economic sphere.

While the policy of social, political and economic separation between race groups in South Africa is founded upon the principle of separate development which is intended to ensure the autonomy of all the groups, it can be seen, in the light of the previous discussion that, in practice, this does not occur and that the system in fact undermines the principle of autonomy in several important ways. Firstly, it is apparent that the separation occurs within the context of a common economy which is controlled by the white group. This means that other race groups are not economically independent and can therefore not be seen as autonomous in any real sense. Secondly, the social segregation of race groups is achieved via a set of legal injunctions which influence almost all aspects of an individual's life including where he may live, how and by whom he may be educated, whom he may marry and even with whom he may associate socially. Thus it is apparent that the individual choices which may be made by members of the society are significantly restricted and individual autonomous action is curtailed by legal prohibitions.

With this admittedly cursory review as a basis, discussion may now proceed to a consideration of the ways in which the socio-political structure of South Africa may influence the mental health of members of South African society and the implications that it has for psychologists in their role as promoters of mental health.

INFLUENCES ON MENTAL HEALTH

Much debate continues about the factors which constitute the set causes of the universal problem of 'mental illness' or psychological maladjustment. While there is undoubtedly an organic basis to many types of mental illness, particularly in its extreme forms such as psychosis, it is also apparent that optimal psychological development and well-being is hampered by conditions that pertain within most human societies. Simply put, there is inevitably a conflict between the individual's desire to satisfy his basic needs and achieve his individual aspirations and the societal conditions and demands which impede this achievement. Of course, both individual aspirations and the impediments to the achievement of these aspirations differ across societies and the degree and nature of the resulting conflicts and frustrations within individuals will

100

therefore also differ. However, Maslow (1954) has constructed a hierarchy of human needs which he proposes as universal and therefore common to all societies. It may be useful therefore to employ his model as a framework within which to discuss some of the major factors operative in South African society which may hamper the development of optimal psychological well-being in all the members of this society.

Maslow's theory identifies nine categories of human needs and aspirations and arranges them in a hierarchical ordering. Individuals must satisfy the more basic needs before aspiring to the satisfaction of other higher order needs. Figure 3 illustrates the ranking of these needs and aspirations.

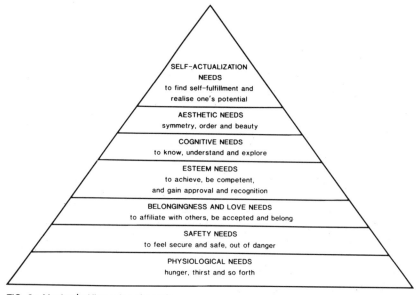

FIG. 3 : Maslow's Hierarchy of needs.

In all societies, individual members will be located at different points of the hierarchy and will therefore have differing aspirations, with the degree of economic wealth, development and advancement of the society as a whole determining the level at which the majority of individuals are located. In South Africa, with the differential allocation of economic benefits, the level at which the majority of the white population is located can be expected to be higher than the level of the other groups. Thus, for example, while the white population group generally has both its physiological and safety needs recognized, this is not necessarily the case for the other groups who are not similarly advantaged within the system. To discuss the effects of South African society on the fulfilment of individual needs as though all groups were located at the same level may, therefore, constitute a distortion of the social reality of the country. As the white population group, due to its access to superior facilities, enjoys a standard of living comparable to that of Western countries such as the United States of America and Great Britain, and as the autonomy of individual members of this group is consequently less restricted, the socio-political situation in this country may be seen as having fewer implications for the satisfaction of needs within this group. For this reason, discussion of the implications of this system for psychological well-being will be confined to the other population groups, who, it must also be remembered, constitute the majority of the inhabitants of the country.

Prior to this discussion, the effects of being unable to achieve aspirations at whatever level they are located should be considered. Within Maslow's theory, full psychological development and well-being can only be realized once more basic needs have been satisfied. In other words optimal mental and emotional functioning is possible only at the top end of the hierarchy. If an individual has been prevented at any level from moving upwards in the hierarchy one can expect a degree of psychological distress arising out of the frustration he must inevitably experience. This distress may take the form of a number of psychological symptoms including depression, anxiety and alcoholism. It can be expected, therefore, that the prevalence of psychological problems within a society is to some extent influenced by the degree to which individuals within the society are able to realize the aspirations of the level on which they are operating. The remaining part of this section will consider the hindrances to the realization of these aspirations experienced by the black population of South Africa. It must be emphasized, of course, that not all individual black inhabitants of the country are located at the same levels of the hierarchy, but there are certain common difficulties experienced by individuals at each level which arise out of the societal context of the country. The hindrances at each level will therefore be discussed separately.

1. *Physiological and Safety Needs*

The needs of individuals at these levels may be broadly categorized as needs for adequate food, housing, health and material security. It is apparent that the satisfaction of these needs depends upon the availability of employment which can provide sufficient monetary gain to provide these necessities. In South Africa, such gainful employment is not ensured for all members of society with a high unemployment rate (the most recent estimate being 407 000 unemployed black people, with unofficial statistics making this number much higher) and with many of those who are employed earning wages which are insufficient. In 1975 it was calculated that 30% of black families were earning below the poverty datum line (calculated at R91 – R120 per month) and only

102

32% of black families had an income of over R200 per month. Thus, the acquisition of adequate material security is problematic for many of the black population. Housing represents an additional problem, particularly in the urban areas where black families are restricted to allocated residential areas and are dependent on the state to provide adequate housing. The construction of housing has not kept pace with the demand and as a result there is chronic overcrowding in the urban areas with, for example, houses in Soweto built to accommodate 4 people found by a survey conducted in 1981 to be accommodating up to 17 people (Unterhalter, 1982). The lack of privacy and consequent irritability and frustration arising out of such conditions can only be seen as psychologically deleterious.

2. Affiliation Needs

These needs are traditionally satisfied by an individual locating himself within his family and within a broader cohesive community. One of the significant aspects of South African society which militates against such location is the migrant labour system, which necessitates that labourers from rural areas leave their families and live in hostels in urban areas for periods of six months at a time. This disruption of family life has inevitable negative consequences both for the labourers and their families who must, in order to satisfy their basic physiological and safety needs, experience repeated separation from significant members of the family (normally the fathers and older sons). The labourers themselves experience isolation and alienation from supportive social groups, for, while the families remain within their original group, the transient nature of the labourers in the urban areas prevents the formation of satisfactory alternative affiliations and social support systems within this context.

The Group Areas Act, which frequently gives rise to the removal of individuals and families from communities within which they have been established to newly constructed housing schemes, is also disruptive to this necessary process of the establishment of mutually supportive community affiliations.

3. Esteem Needs

These needs are necessarily connected to the perception of approval and recognition by others, which gives the individual a measure by which to assign himself value. There appear to be two major factors which for the black person would undermine the development of self-esteem. Firstly, it has been noted that there is a high degree of social separation between race groups and that this separation is accompanied by the unequal distribution of social benefits. Particularly in urban areas where there is a high degree of contact between

103

members of different race groups, this differential allocation is patently obvious as is the fact that the facilities and services available to members of the white group are inevitably superior. Prolonged exposure to social situations in which one is allocated an apparently inferior status must interfere with the development of both group and individual self-esteem. This is possibly because rewards are traditionally allocated on the basis of value and worth and the reception of inferior rewards implies inferior value or worth within a society. The second major factor to be considered is that, in Westernized societies, social status is often associated with economic status and accorded on the basis of economic productivity and gains. Due to such factors as inferior education, job allocation and reluctance to train and employ black people as skilled members of the economy (because of the desire to maintain such positions for the white population whose employment would otherwise be jeopardised), it is difficult for many black workers to achieve such economic status and they are therefore restricted to some degree, to lower status employment and thereby to lower social status.

4. Cognitive Needs

In order to satisfy these relatively higher order needs, the major necessity is adequate educational facilities. Once again, the demand for these facilities amongst the black population exceeds the rate at which they are provided and education for the black population is therefore inferior and conducted in inferior surroundings, with overcrowding and understaffing of schools. The inferior quality of the education received by blacks makes it difficult for many to cope with the high standard demanded at universities and thereby restricts the number of black people who manage to enter the professions to which they may aspire.

5. Aesthetic and Self-actualization Needs

It is understood that the achievement of these needs depends on the satisfaction of the previously discussed more basic human needs and it will be apparent from the previous discussion that the number of black South Africans who can aspire to these is limited. Indeed, if it is assumed that these needs depend on the capacity for autonomous decision-making and action, it is doubtful that the number of South Africans of any race who can reach these levels is more than a small minority, but the denial of political and economic freedom experienced by the black population must imply that the proportion of this population which reaches these levels is significantly lower than that of the white population.

The cumulative effect of these social impediments to psychological development in South Africa implies that there must be a significant degree of psychological stress within the black population. South African psychologists are therefore faced with a large number of people who potentially could benefit from their services. The obvious needs are for services which can both prevent the development of psychological problems and treat them when they do arise. However, in attempting to achieve both the prevention and cure of these problems, psychologists in South Africa are confronted by socio-political factors which are similar to those which have been described as contributing to the cause of these problems. These factors will be discussed later in this chapter and will be considered from the points of view of the psychologist in relation to the society as a whole, to the mental health institutions within the country and to individual clients.

MULTI-CULTURAL COMPOSITION OF THE POPULATION

The development of particular individual values and attitudes is influenced by a variety of factors, one of the most significant being the cultural milieu within which the individual is located. Cultural background determines, amongst other things, the nature of social hierarchies, accepted social roles and channels of communication, and basic beliefs about the relationship between man and the environment. Important differences may therefore be expected to exist between individuals with differing cultural backgrounds.

The profession of psychology developed in the Western cultural system and therefore its basic assumptions about the nature of man, as well as the ethical principles which it holds as of primary importance are specifically Western in origin. As a result, psychologists may experience difficulties in understanding and working effectively with members of other cultural groups, whose assumptions and values may be significantly different. The nature of these difficulties and possible solutions to them should be areas of special concern for South African psychologists who, as has been pointed out, are working within a multi-cultural society in which the majority of the population originate from indigenous African cultural backgrounds. In this section, the major aspects of the cultural diversity in South Africa which are potentially problematic for South African psychologists will be briefly considered, while the specific influences of these factors on the psychologist's work in mental institutions and with individual clients will be discussed in the following section.

The first and most obvious difficulty encountered by white psychologists in working with black population groups is the language barrier that may exist. The two official languages in South Africa are those of the white population groups while the language spoken by black South Africans will be determined by the tribal stem to which they belong. Education in the official languages is compulsory in the school systems of all population groups and most black people living in urban areas will be able to communicate in either one or both of these languages. However, there are significant differences in the semantic and syntactic structure of the 'white' and 'black' languages which may mean that certain concepts important to the rural black population cannot be expressed in English or Afrikaans while some English and Afrikaans words, (e.g. the word 'depressed') do not have corresponding referents in many black languages. This may lead to misunderstandings and misinterpretations between white psychologists and black clients. While it is desirable that white psychologists who work with black clients be able to speak and understand the language of their clients this may be an ambitious project, in that, as has been seen, the language spoken by the black population varies between areas within the country (so that, for example, in the Cape, Xhosa is the predominant language, while in Natal, Zulu is more common and Sotho predominates in the Transvaal). This means that a psychologist who can speak the indigenous black language in one area of the country will not necessarily be able to communicate with black clients in another area. Many psychologists work with interpreters if their black clients cannot speak English or Afrikaans, but Cheetham and Griffiths (1981) have experienced difficulties with this as urbanized interpreters are occasionally embarrassed by the rural beliefs of some patients. They therefore do not always interpret the communications of the patient accurately. It does seem, however, that, to facilitate communication with black clients, white psychologists must have a rudimentary understanding of the language spoken by these clients and be particularly aware of language usage (for example the extensive use of metaphorical expression) which may confuse a clear understanding of the client's communications. It is also important to remember that the cultural beliefs of black clients will be embedded in their language.

The fundamental differences between the Western culture of the psychologist and traditional African cultures have been fairly well documented (Bührmann, 1977(a), 1977(b), 1979; Schweitzer and Bührmann, 1978; Awanbor, 1982; Fischer, 1962; Cheetham and Griffiths, 1981). The major factor which has been identified by these authors as significant in determining differences in outlook and thereby constituting a potential barrier to accurate understanding of clients by the psychologist, is the difference in the interpretation of causality in these two cultures. While psychologists attribute the origins of psychological or behavioural maladjustment to essentially human factors, within traditional cultures these are attributed to factors which are non-human – normally the spirits of the ancestors. Thus, while the psychologist would concentrate on changing the individual's perception of and relationship to other people or the broader social environment, traditional healers advise their clients on how to placate the ancestors in order to restore equilibrium within the individual. In addition to this basic difference in orientation, the

106

psychologist must also be aware of the social customs and norms existing in traditional cultural systems which determine the ways in which the individual may express emotions or assert himself in relation to others. For example, what may be interpreted by a psychologist as unassertive behaviour may well be regarded as appropriately assertive within the individual's culture (Dowdall, 1982). It would be difficult, if not impossible, for psychologists to familiarize themselves with all the customs arising out of the traditional cultures in the country and, indeed, doing so may not be helpful in work with individual clients as particular customs vary between sub-groups within the same broad cultural group. However, sensitivity to the influence of customary practice on client's behaviour is essential.

In South Africa, the difficulties of working with members of other cultural groups are further complicated by the fact that the black population group may be seen as being in a process of transition, adapting their traditional cultures in the presence of the Western culture of the white population. This process can be attributed to the fact that, as is apparent from discussion in the previous section, the white group is dominant in all aspects of South African society and its cultural system has therefore also become dominant. Through the rapidly accelerating processes of urbanization and industrialization which have made a significant impact on all communities within the country, the Western culture of the white group has concomitantly interfaced with and influenced the traditional cultures. Furthermore, because of the extent of inter-cultural contact, it is impossible to speak of any distinct cultural group in isolation.

Members of the black population group vary in the degree of their acceptance of traditional beliefs and customs. Those who are still strongly influenced by these values live mainly in the rural areas, while those in the urban areas may be regarded as operating primarily within Western culture. Thus, it may not be assumed that traditional customs and beliefs exert an equal influence on all black clients and to do so would be both simplistic and detrimental to effective work with these clients. Extra sensitivity is therefore required by psychologists as to the ways in which traditional cultural practices may influence black clients and the extent to which they in fact do influence each individual client.

A final point about this process of change apart from the complications that it adds to the psychologist's attempts to understand black clients, is the potential effect that it has on the mental health of the members of the black population who are in this process of transition. These effects have been considered by, amongst others, Gijana and Louw (1981) and O'Connell (1980), who point out that the process of urbanization which exposes people to a different culture and forces them to live within this culture may lead to feelings of alienation and isolation as traditional practices are seen to be inappropriate and ineffective within a Western society. A period of adjustment is therefore inevitable and may involve conflict and psychological distress within the individual, which impairs his functioning in a highly demanding social situation. The higher incidence of mental disorder in urbanized blacks is attributed to these difficulties in adjustment, but O'Connell points out that there has been a concomitantly higher incidence of 'thwasa' (a Xhosa psychological condition, difficult to categorize within Western nosology) amongst rural Xhosa women who are exposed to higher stress as the men leave the rural areas to seek work in the towns.

The process of transition of the black population may therefore increase the likelihood of mental disorder in the black population and certainly complicates the understanding of this population by white psychologists, who may view these people as neither entirely rooted within their traditional cultures nor as entirely Westernized.

INFLUENCES ON THE PRACTICE OF CLINICAL PSYCHOLOGY

The Psychologist and Society

In chapter three it was seen that much debate still centres on the question of whether psychologists as professionals should be concerned not only with the treatment of mental disorder but also with its prevention by challenging the societal factors which cause psychological malfunctioning. This debate is not near resolution at the present time, but the issues involved in it need to be considered within the South African context. It has been pointed out that in all societies some degree of frustration of needs and resultant psychological distress exists and that some of the frustrating mechanisms are similar to those operating in South Africa. For example, the psychological negative effects of racial discrimination have long been a source of concern to psychologists in America and there, as here, the question arises as to whether psychologists should actively oppose such discrimination. The crucial difference between the American and South African societies is, however, that in the former racial discrimination is a social custom whereas in the latter this discrimination constitutes state policy. Actively opposing this discrimination in South Africa therefore involves opposition to the state and can be construed as a political stand, whereas this is not necessarily the case elsewhere. There therefore exists a perhaps realistic fear that should one's opposition to the state policy of racial discrimination be perceived as too active and vigorous and thereby constitute a threat to the security of the current government, legal measures may be employed against one, whether or not this opposition was motivated by professional concern for the health of inhabitants of the country. However, this does not mean that such professional concern cannot be expressed and, in fact, if it is accepted that certain aspects of the state policy are detrimental to mental health, it may well be an ethical obligation of the South African psychologist to bring this to the attention of the authorities by conducting research which will illuminate the extent of the detrimental influences and the implications that these have for the functioning of the society as a whole.

The Psychologist in Mental Health Institutions

The problems experienced by South African psychologists within mental hospitals may be seen as caused both by the socio-political dispensation within the country which negatively influences the quality of facilities and treatment available to black patients and by language and cultural differences which complicate understanding and treatment of mental disorders in these patients.

While there are 9 954 beds in mental hospitals assigned to white patients, there are 9 068 beds assigned for black patients (Dept. of Constitutional Development and Planning, 1980). In view of the fact that the black population is four times larger than the white population, this allocation of beds means that black mental hospitals are frequently overcrowded and understaffed. This frequently results in premature discharge and a high turnover rate of patients which makes effective therapy and management of therapeutic ward programmes a difficult task. As a result, the psychologist's role within the institution is often confined to that of diagnostician with the emphasis being on pharmacological management of patients. It is in the area of accurate diagnosis that language and cultural differences became important in mental institutions. Cheetham and Griffiths (1981) and Bührmann (1977a) have pointed to the disproportionate number of black patients who are diagnosed as schizophrenic within mental institutions. They suggest that this number may not in fact be reflective of the actual incidence of schizophrenia in this population but may reflect errors in diagnosis arising out of a failure to distinguish culturally determined communication and behaviour from symptoms of schizophrenia. This would suggest that extra care should be taken in diagnosing patients in whom language and cultural differences may create barriers to accurate understanding. The extra care necessary implies that more time should be spent with these patients determining which aspects of their behaviour and communication are culturally based and which may be indicative of mental disorder but it is precisely this extra time which is not available within black mental hospitals due to the factors mentioned above. The result of overcrowding frequently means that black patients are allocated less time for diagnosis and assessment than are white patients and if this results, as Cheetham and Griffiths suggest, in inaccurate diagnosis of these patients, they will be receiving incorrect treatment. In chapter three it was pointed out that one of the basic rights of patients in mental hospitals, whose autonomy has been significantly curtailed, is the right to adequate treatment. All of the above discussion points to the problem that in many cases this basic right is not accorded to black patients.

The question arises as to what the psychologists in South Africa may do to alleviate this problem. The negative aspects of black mental hospitals are frequently attributed to the differential allocation of funds for health services for blacks and regarded as being a result of state policy and therefore beyond the powers of the individual psychologist to change. However, psychologists may achieve some gains in this area by pressing for reforms within the institutions in which they work. Research into the nature and degree of the inadequacies of the institution and the effects that these have upon the adequacy of mental health care may carry some weight, and reports on this research could be forwarded both to the authorities of the institution and to the political and bureaucratic authorities responsible for these institutions, such as the Department of Health and Welfare. Sufficient concern expressed by a significant number of mental health workers may result in the pressure necessary for reforms to be instituted by these authorities.

The Psychologist and Individual Clients

The problem of working with clients who belong to different race groups and who therefore have a different cultural background and experience differential social benefits is certainly not unique to South Africa and has been a subject of concern to American psychologists as well (e.g. Mizio, 1972; Kadushin, 1972). The difficulties inherent in working across race and cultural lines in psychotherapy can be roughly divided into difficulties in establishing an adequate therapeutic relationship and difficulties in defining and achieving therapeutic goals.

In establishing an effective therapeutic relationship, two major factors seem to be important. The first is a degree of trust in the therapist, while the second is a recognition that the task of achieving therapeutic goals is one which is shared equally by the therapist and client. Kruger (1980) writes: 'Within this relationship the reality of the client as a person can emerge but the client's consciousness of his own reality is always co-constituted by the consciousness of his relationship with the therapist' (p. 26). At this point it seems necessary to consider what aspects of the black client's relationship with the white therapist may be affected by the particular societal circumstances of South Africa. Firstly, as Kadushin (1972) points out, in societies where racism and its effects are prominent for the black person, the establishment of trust in the therapist who as a white person may represent a feared and resented group of oppressors, presents immediate difficulties. Racial segregation fosters racial stereotypes in both participants and the therapist may have to be aware that what he may experience as resistance on the part of the client may reflect a more basic difficulty in accepting that the therapist is genuinely concerned with his well-being and has an interest in him as an autonomous person. Fibush and Turnquest (1970) address this problem and suggest that one way to combat it is to introduce the question of race and the client's feelings and fantasies about the therapist as a member of the 'opposite' race at an early point in the therapy. Through their research they found that tackling these issues early on in the therapeutic process made the establishment of a good relationship and, thereby, effective therapeutic work easier for both therapist and client.

The second issue inherent in the therapeutic relationship is the question of the balance of power. It has been seen that clients of any race frequently approach the therapist as an authority who will be able to remove their suffering by exercising his expertise. One of the initial tasks of therapy and one of the first steps on the road to autonomy within the client is to reduce this expectation and lead the client to take more responsibility for changing within the therapeutic process. In South Africa the superior status of the therapist as an expert is exacerbated by his superior social status by virtue of being a member of the white group. Many black clients will have been accustomed to assuming a passive inferior role in relation to white people who they normally encounter in situations where the white person is an authority who makes all the decisions. The process of moving such clients towards a position where they are in a more equal relationship to the therapist is therefore made more problematic and it may be possible that the therapist will need to take a directive role for longer than usual, gradually allowing the client to assume more and more responsibility. This need to be initially directive may be especially important with clients who are strongly based in the traditional culture and are more familiar with traditional healers who assume a very powerful and directive role in relation to their clients.

The difficulties of defining and achieving therapeutic goals may also stem from both socio-political and cultural origins. Firstly, in many cases the psychological distress of the client may be seen as attributable to or at least aggravated by the circumstances outlined in the socio-political section of this chapter. It has been seen that these circumstances arise out of a complex legal structure and are therefore minimally amenable to change by either the therapist or the client. In many cases, therefore, the client may be prevented from making changes in his environment which would reduce the negative consequences he is experiencing. It has been seen that the purpose of therapy is not to help clients to adjust to adverse circumstances, but to remove the barriers which hamper autonomous action and thereby hamper the client's ability to change these circumstances. However, the fostering of the capacity for autonomous action in clients may have limited success in a society such as

111

South Africa in which, as has been seen, certain types of autonomous action may be legally restricted.

In addition, the psychologist needs to be aware that the expression of autonomy may vary in different cultures and must avoid losing the client or causing unnecessary conflict within him by forcing upon him his own Western definition of autonomy. In chapter three the danger of imposing values and goals on a client was indicated and this is particularly important where the client's cultural background may determine that his value system is significantly different from that of the therapist. In working with black clients the therapist must be especially aware of the possibility that such basic differences exist and, where necessary, must be prepared to explore with the client what the significant aspects of his culture are, and where the client perceives himself as an individual in relation to these aspects. This approach is not fundamentally different to the approach which should be taken with any client, but possibly more sensitivity is needed to this aspect of the therapeutic process and the therapist should more strongly guard against assuming commonality of values and attitudes where these may not exist.

CONCLUSION

In this chapter the particular social circumstances in South Africa which have bearing upon the efficient functioning of psychologists within the country have been briefly analysed. While many of these circumstances are not unique to this country and problems of racial discrimination and cultural differences are common to most countries, both of these problems are exacerbated in South Africa by a legally enforced policy of racial segregation. Although the problems of changing the system are considerable, it does seem, however, that psychologists as professionals may have a role to play in constantly alerting societal authorities to the negative effects that some practices have on the psychologist's area of concern, i.e. the healthy psychological development and functioning of all the members of society.

BIBLIOGRAPHY

American Psychological Association, 'Ethical standards of psychologists', *American Psychologist*, 36:6 (1981): 633-638.

American Psychological Association, 'Ethical standards for research with Human Subjects', *APA Monitor*, (May 1972): 1-XIX.

American Psychological Association, 'Revised ethics principles adopted', *APA Monitor*, 4:1 (1973):2.

Anastasi, A., *Psychological Testing*, 3rd edn., New York, Macmillan, 1976.

Anderten, Patricia, Staulcup, Valerie and Grisso, Thomas, 'On being ethical in legal places', *Professional Psychology*, II:5 (October 1980): 764-773.

Annitto, William and Kass, Walter, 'Psychotherapy, psychopharmacology and the illusion of curing', *Bulletin of the Menninger Clinic*, 43:6 (1979): 552-555.

Awanbor, D., 'The healing process in African psychotherapy', *American Journal of Psychotherapy*, 36:2 (April 1982): 206-213.

Ayllon, T. and Skuban, W., 'Accountability in psychotherapy: a test case', *Behaviour Therapy & Experimental Psychiatry*, 4: (1973): 19-30.

Barnhouse, R. T., 'Sex between patient and therapist', *Journal of the American Academy of Psychoanalysis*, 6:4 (1978): 533-546.

Barron, J., 'A prolegomenon to the personality of the psychotherapist: choices and changes', *Psychotherapy, Theory Research and Practice*, 15:4, (Winter 1978): 309-313.

Bartholomew, A. A., Badger, P. and Milte, K. L., 'The psychologist as an expert witness in the criminal courts', *Australian Psychologist*, 12:2 (July 1977): 133-150.

Bastiansen, S., 'Psychotherapy and the autonomy of the individual', *Psychotherapy & Psychosomatics*, 24:4-6 (1974): 399-404.

Bazelon, D. L., 'The perils of wizardry', *American Journal of Psychiatry*, 131:12 (December 1974): 1317-1322.

Bazelon, D. L., 'A jurist's view of psychiatry', *Journal of Psychiatry and Law*, 3:2 (1975): 175-190.

Beauchamp, T. L. and Childress, J. F., *Principles of Biomedical Ethics*, 2nd edn., New York, Oxford University Press, 1983.

Bergin, A. E., 'Psychotherapy can be dangerous', *Psychology Today*, (November 1975): 96-104.

Bersoff, D. N., 'Therapists as protectors and policemen: new roles as a result of Tarasoff', *Professional Psychology*, 7:3 (August 1976): 267-273.

Beutler, L. E., 'Values, beliefs, religion and the persuasive influence of psychotherapy', *Psychotherapy, Theory, Research and Practice*, 16:4 (Winter 1979): 432-441.

Bloch, S. and Chodoff, P., *Psychiatric Ethics*, London, Oxford University Press, 1981.

Braginsky, D. D. and Braginsky, B.M., 'Psychologists: high priests of the middle class', *Psychology Today*, (December 1973): 15-20, 138-140.

Breggin, P. R., 'Psychotherapy as applied ethics', *Psychiatry*, 34 (February 1971): 59-75.

Brodsky, S. L. and Robey, A., 'On becoming an expert witness: issues of orientation and effectiveness', *Professional Psychology*, 3 (1972): 173-176.

Brown, E. C., 'Usuriousness and Psychotherapy', *Psychotherapy: Theory, Research and Practice*, 17:4 (Winter 1980): 420-424.

Bugental, J. T. F., 'The humanistic ethic, the individual in psychotherapy as a societal change agent', *Journal of Humanistic Psychology*, 11 (Spring 1971): 11-25.

Bührmann, M. V., 'Western psychiatry and the Xhosa patient', *South African Medical Journal*, 51 (1977a): 464-466.

Bührmann, M. V., 'Xhosa diviners as psychotherapists', *Psychotherapeia*, 3:4 (1977b): 17-20.

Bührmann, M. V., 'Why are certain procedures of the indigenous healers effective?' *Psychotherapeia*, 5:3 (July 1979): 20-25.

113

Cahn, C. H., 'The ethics of involuntary treatment: the position of the Canadian Psychiatric Association', *Canadian Journal of Psychiatry*, 27:1 (February 1982): 67–74.

Cheetham, R. W. S. and Griffiths, J. A., 'Errors in the diagnosis of schizophrenia in black and Indian patients', *South African Medical Journal*, 59 (January 1981): 71–75.

Cohen, R. J. and Smith, F. J., 'Socially reinforced obsessing: etiology of a disorder in a Christian Scientist', *Journal of Consulting and Clinical Psychology*, 44 (1976): 142–144.

Coyne, J. C., 'The place of informed consent in ethical dilemmas', *Journal of Consulting and Clinical Psychology*, 44:6 (1976): 1015–1017.

Coyne, J. C. and Widiger, T. A., 'Toward a participatory model of psychotherapy', *Professional Psychology*, (1978): 701–711.

Davidson, V., 'Psychiatry's problem with no name: therapist-patient sex', *The American Journal of Psychoanalysis*, 37 (1977): 43–51.

Denkowski, K. M. and Denkowski, G. C., 'Client-counsellor confidentiality: an update of rationale, legal status, and implications', *Personnel and Guidance Journal*, 60:6 (February 1982: 371–375.

Donaldson case: see *Prettyman, E. B. Jr.* and *Snyder, A. R.*

Dowdall, T., 'Behaviour therapy in South Africa: a review', *Journal of Behavior Therapy and Experimental Psychiatry*, 13 (1982): 279–286.

Dubey, J., 'Confidentiality as a requirement of the therapist: technical necessities for absolute privilege in psychotherapy', *American Journal of Psychiatry*, 131:10 (October 1974): 1093–1096.

Eisner, M. S., 'Ethical problems in social psychological experimentation in the laboratory', *Canadian Psychological Review*, 18:3 (July 1977): 233–241.

Ellis, A., 'The value of efficiency in psychotherapy', *Psychotherapy: Theory, Research & Practice*, 17:4 (1980): 414–419.

Engelhardt, H. T., 'Psychotherapy as meta-ethics', *Psychiatry*, 36:4 (November 1973): 440–445.

Ennis, B. J. and Litwack, T. R., 'Psychiatry and the presumption of expertise – flipping coins in the courtroom', *California Law Review*, 62 (1974) 693–753.

Epstein, G. N., 'Informed consent and the dyadic relationship', *Journal of Psychiatry and Law*, 6:3 (Fall 1978): 359–362.

Fibush, E. and Turnquest, B., 'A black and white approach to the problem of racism', *Social Casework*, 51 (October 1970): 459–466.

Fink, A. M. and Butcher, J. M., 'Reducing objections to personality inventories with special instructions', *Educational and Psychological Measurement*, 32 (1972): 631–639.

Finney, J. C., 'Therapist and patient after hours', *American Journal of Psychotherapy*, 29:4 (October 1975): 593–603.

Fischer, P. J., 'Cultural aspects of Bantu psychiatry', *South African Medical Journal*, 36:8 (February 1962): 133–138.

Foster, H. H. Jr., 'The conflict and reconciliation of the ethical interests of therapist and patient', *Journal of Psychiatry and Law*, 3:1 (1975): 39–48.

Garfield, S. L., 'An issue in psychotherapy: comments on a case study', *Journal of Abnormal Psychology*, 83:2 (1974): 202–203.

Gijana, E. W. M. and Louw, J., 'Psychiatric disorders in a developing community as reflected by archival material', *South African Medical Journal*, 59 (June 1981): 988–991.

Government Gazette, No. R437, (March 1979, September 1977).

Graham, S. R., 'Values in Psychotherapy', *Psychotherapy: Theory, Research and Practice*, 17:4 (1980): 396.

Graziano, A. M. and Fink, R. S., 'Second-order effects in mental health treatment', *Journal of Consulting and Clinical Psychology*, 40:3 (1973): 356–364.

Haley, J., *Problem-solving Therapy*, San Francisco, Josey-Bass, 1977: 195–221.

Halleck, S. L., 'Therapy is the handmaiden of the status quo', *Psychology Today*, (April 1971): 30.

Hare, R., 'The philosophical basis of psychiatric ethics', in Bloch, S. and Chodoff, P. (eds.), *Psychiatric Ethics*, London, Oxford University Press, 1981.

Hare-Mustin, R. T., 'Ethical considerations in the use of sexual contact in psychotherapy', *Psychotherapy: Theory, Research and Practice*, 11:4 (Winter 1974): 308–310.

Hare-Mustin, R. T., Marecek, J., Kaplan, A. G. and Liss-Levenson, N., 'Rights of clients, responsibilities of therapists', *American Psychologist*, 34:1 (January 1979): 3–16.

Hays, R. J., 'Sexual contact between psychotherapist and patient: legal remedies', *Psychological Reports*, 47 (1980): 1247–1254.

Helmchen, H. and Muller-Oerlinghausen, B., 'The inherent paradox of clinical trials in psychiatry', *Journal of Medical Ethics*, 1 (1975): 170–172.

Hurvitz, N., 'Psychotherapy as a means of social control', *Journal of Consulting and Clinical Psychology*, 40:2 (1973): 232–239.

Jensen, A. R., *Educability and Group Differences*, New York, Harper and Row, 1973.

Kadushin, A., 'The racial factor in the interview', *Social Work NY*, 17 (May 1972): 88–98.

Karasu, T. B., 'The ethics of psychotherapy', *American Journal of Psychiatry*, 137:12 (December 1980): 1502–1511.

Kardener, S. H., 'Sex and the physician-patient relationship', *American Journal of Psychiatry*, 131:10 (October 1974): 1134–1136.

Kennedy, W. M., 'Implications for counselling from Erich Fromm's view of man's ethical responsibility', *Dissertation Abstracts International*, 34:5-B (November 1973): 2307–2308.

Kisch, J. and Kroll, Jerome, 'Meaningfulness versus effectiveness – paradoxical implications in the evaluation of psychotherapy', *Psychotherapy: Theory, Research and Practice*, 17:4 (Winter 1980): 400–413.

Knapp, S. and Vandecreek, L., 'Tarasoff; five years later', *Professional Psychology*, 13:4 (1982): 511–516.

Kopolow, L. E., 'A review of major implications of the O'Connor v. Donaldson decision', *American Journal of Psychiatry*, 133:4 (April 1976): 379–383.

Kruger, D., 'The white therapist and the black client – a problem of cross-cultural contact', *Psychotherapeia*, 6:3 (July 1980): 25–32.

Lane, P. J. and Spruill, J., 'To tell or not to tell: the psychotherapist's dilemma', *Psychotherapy: Theory, Research and Practice*, 17:2 (Summer 1980): 202–209.

Lederer, W., 'Some moral dilemmas encountered in psychotherapy' *Psychiatry*, 34 (February 1971): 75–85.

Leifer, R., 'The psychiatrist and tests of criminal responsibility', *American Psychologist*, 19 (1964): 825–830.

Leland, J., ' "Invasion" of the body?' *Psychotherapy: Theory, Research and Practice*, 13:3 (Fall 1976): 214–219.

Loftus, E. and Monahan, J., 'Trial by data: psychological research as legal evidence', *American Psychologist*, 35:3 (March 1980): 270–283.

Lowental, U., 'The vicissitudes of discretion in psychotherapy', *American Journal of Psychotherapy*, 28:2 (April 1974): 235–243.

Maloney, M. P. and Ward, M. P., *Psychological Assessment: a Conceptual Approach*, New York, Oxford University Press, 1976.

Mariner, A. S., 'The problem of therapeutic privacy', *Psychiatry*, 30:1 (1967): 60–72.

Maslow, A. H., *Motivation and Personality*, New York, Harper and Row, 1954.

McLemore, C. W. and Court, J. H., 'Religion and psychotheraphy – ethics, civil liberties, and clinical savvy; a critique', *Journal of Consulting and Clinical Psychology*, 45:6 (1977): 1172–1175.

Milgram, S., 'Behavioural study of obedience', *Journal of Abnormal and Social Psychology*, 67 (1963): 371–378.

Miller, D. and Burt, R. A., 'Children's rights on entering therapeutic institutions', *Child and Youth Services*, 4:1-2 (1982): 89-98.

Mizio, E., 'White worker - minority client', *Social Work NY*, 17 (May 1972): 82-86.

Morse, S. J., 'Law and mental health professionals: the limits of expertise', *Professional Psychology*, (August 1978): 389-399.

Nichols, J. F., 'The marital family therapist as an expert witness: some thoughts and suggestions', *Journal of Marital and Family Therapy*, 6:3 (July 1980): 293-299.

Noll, J. O., 'The psychotherapist and informed consent', *American Journal of Psychiatry*, 133:12 (December 1976): 1451-1453.

Nye, S., 'Commentary on model law on confidentiality of health and social service records', *American Journal of Psychiatry*, 136 (1979): 145.

O'Connell, M. C., 'The aetiology of thwasa', *Psychotherapeia*, 6:4 (October 1980): 18-23.

O'Leary, D. K. and Borkovec, T. D., 'Conceptual methodological and ethical problems of placebo groups in psychotherapy research', *American Psychologist*, (September 1978): 821-831.

Pacht, A. R., Kuehn, J. K., Bassett, H. T. and Nash, M. M., 'The current status of the psychologist as an expert witness', *Professional Psychology*, 4 (1973): 409-413.

Parker, L., 'Psychotherapy and ethics', *Cornell Journal of Social Relations*, 9:2 (Fall 1974): 207-216.

Plaut, E. A., 'A perspective on confidentiality', *American Journal of Psychiatry*, 131:9 (September 1974): 1021-1024.

Pope, K. S., Simpson, H. S. and Weiner, M. F., 'Malpractice in outpatient psychotherapy', *American Journal of Psychotherapy*, 32:4 (October 1978): 593-601.

Poythress, N. G., 'Mental health expert testimony: current problems', *Journal of Psychiatry and Law*, 5 (1977): 201-227.

Poythress, N. G. Jr., 'Psychiatric expertise in civil commitment: training attorneys to cope with expert testimony', *Law and Human Behaviour*, 2:1 (1978): 1-23.

Prettyman, E. B. Jr. and Snyder, A. R., 'Amicus curiae in the Donaldson case', *American Journal of Psychiatry*, 132:1 (January 1975): 109-115.

Rachlin, S., Pam, A. and Milton, J., 'Civil liberties versus involuntary hospitalization', *American Journal of Psychiatry*, 132:2 (February 1975): 189-192.

Reisman, J. M., *The Development of Clinical Psychology*, New York, Appleton Century Crofts, 1966.

Reiss, D., Costell, R. and Almond, R., 'Personal needs, values and technical preferences in the psychiatric hospital', *Archives of General Psychiatry*, 33 (July 1976): 795-804.

Resnick, J. H. and Schwartz, T., 'Ethical Standards as an independent variable in psychological research', *American Psychologist*, (February 1973): 134-139.

Robinson, D. N., 'Harm, offense and nuisance', *American Psychologist*, (April 1974): 232-239.

Robitscher, J., 'The impact of new legal standards on psychiatry or who are David Bazelon and Thomas Szasz and why are they saying such terrible things about us? or authoritarianism versus nihilism in legal psychiatry', *Journal of Psychiatry and Law*, 3:2 (1975): 410-417.

Robitscher, J., 'Informed consent for psychoanalysis', *Journal of Psychiatry and Law*, 6:3 (Fall 1978): 363-370.

Roll, S. and Millen, L., 'A guide to violating an injunction in psychotherapy: on seeing acquaintances as patients', *Psychotherapy: Theory, Research and Practice*, 18:2 (1981): 178-186.

Rosen, C., 'Why clients relinquish their rights to privacy under sign-away pressures' *Professional Psychology*, (February 1977): 17-25.

Ross, W. D., *The Right and the Good*, Oxford, Clarendon Press, 1930.

Rotter, J. B., *Clinical Psychology*, New Jersey, Prentice-Hall, 1964.

Rugg, E. A., 'Ethical judgements of social research involving experimental deception', *Social Psychology*, (1976).

Sadoff, R. L., 'Informed consent, confidentiality and privilege in psychiatry: practical applications', *Bulletin of the American Academy of Psychiatry and the Law*, 2:2 (June 1974): 101–106.

Schwebel, M., 'Why? unethical practice', *Journal of Counselling Psychology*, 2:2 (1955): 122–128.

Schweitzer, R. D. and Bührmann, M. V., 'An existential-phenomenological interpretation of thwasa among the Xhosa', *Psychotherapeia*, 4:2 (April 1978): 15–18.

Schwitzgebel, K. R., 'A contractual model for the protection of the rights of institutionalized mental patients', *American Psychologist*, (August 1975): 814–821.

Serban, G., 'Sexual activity in therapy: legal and ethical issues', *American Journal of Psychotherapy*, XXXV:1 (1981): 76–85.

Shah, S. A., 'Dangerousness and civil commitment of the mentally ill: some public policy considerations, *American Journal of Psychiatry*, 132:5 (May 1975): 501–505.

Sieghart, P., 'Professional ethics – for whose benefit?' *Journal of Medical Ethics*, 8 (1982): 25–32.

Simon, C. G., 'Psychology and the "Treatment rights movement" ', *Professional Psychology*, 6:3 (August 1975): 243–251.

Singer, J. L., 'The scientific basis of psychotherapeutic practice: a question of values and ethics', *Psychotherapy: Theory, Research and Practice*, 17:4 (Winter 1980): 372–383.

Smith, D. and Peterson, J. A., 'Counselling and values in a time perspective', *Personnel and Guidance Journal*, 55:6 (February 1977): 309–318.

Solomon, P., Kleeman, S. T. and Curran, W. J., 'Confidentiality in psychiatric screening for security clearance', *American Journal of Psychiatry*, 127:11 (May 1971): 143–145.

Statman, J., 'Community mental health as a pacification programme', *Radical Therapist*, 1 (1970): 14–15.

Stone, A. A., 'The legal implications of sexual activity between psychiatrist and patient', *American Journal of Psychiatry*, 133:10 (October 1976): 1138–1141.

Strupp, H. H., 'On failing one's patient', *Psychotherapy: Theory, Research and Practice*, 12:1 (Spring 1975): 39–41.

Strupp, H. H., 'Humanism and psychotherapy – a personal statement of the therapist's essential values', *Psychotherapy: Theory, Research and Practice*, 17:4 (Winter 1980): 396–401.

Strupp, H. H. and Hadley, S. W., 'A tripartite model of mental health and therapeutic outcomes', *American Psychologist*, (March 1977): 186–197.

Sundberg, N. D. and Tyler, L. E., *Clinical Psychology*, London, Methuen, 1963, Chapter 12: 474–489.

Teichner, V. J., 'Psychoanalytic, ethical and legal aspects of confidentiality', *Journal of the American Academy of Psychoanalysis*, 3:3 (July 1975): 293–300.

Unterhalter, B., 'The health of the urban black in the South African context', *Journal of Social Science and Medicine*, 16 (1982): 1111–1117.

Weisskopf-Joelson, E., 'Values: the enfant terrible of psychotherapy', *Psychotherapy: Theory, Research and Practice*, 17:4 (Winter 1980): 459–467.

White, M. D. and White, C. A., 'Involuntarily committed patients' constitutional right to refuse treatment: a challenge to psychology', *American Psychologist*, 36:9 (September 1981): 963–971.

Will, O. A. Jr., 'Values and the Psychotherapist', *The American Journal of Psychoanalysis*, 41:3 (1981): 203–213.

Wolman, B. B., *Handbook of Clinical Psychology*, New York, McGraw-Hill, 1965: 1507–1514.

The Working Group in current Medical/Ethical Problems, 'Ethical Problems of repetitive research', *Journal of Medical Ethics*, 3 (1977): 14–17.

Ziskin, J., *Coping with Psychiatric and Psychological Testimony*, 2nd edn., Beverley Hills, The Law and Psychology Press, 1975.

INDEX

119

DATE DUE

MAR 1 8 '91

APR 18 '91

SEP 22 '94

261-2500

Printed
in USA